FRAGMENTA GENEALOGICA

fragmenta Genealogica

Volume 4

~

**FREDERICK
ARTHUR
CRISP**

HERITAGE BOOKS
2010

HERITAGE BOOKS
AN IMPRINT OF HERITAGE BOOKS, INC.

Books, CDs, and more—Worldwide

For our listing of thousands of titles see our website
at
www.HeritageBooks.com

A Facsimile Reprint
Published 2010 by
HERITAGE BOOKS, INC.
Publishing Division
100 Railroad Ave. #104
Westminster, Maryland 21157

Originally Printed at the Private Press of
Frederick Arthur Crisp
1899

International Standard Book Numbers
Paperbound: 978-0-7884-0493-1
Clothbound: 978-0-7884-8438-4

CONTENTS.

DEEDS.

ENTRIES IN BIBLES, &c.

GRANTS OF ARMS.

MONUMENTAL INSCRIPTIONS.

WILLS AND ADMINISTRATIONS.

WOOD-CUTS OF ARMS AND AUTOGRAPHS.

Fragmenta Genealogica.

VOL. IV.

Joslin Family.

1525.

JOHN JOSSLYN of high Rodyng in the Countie of Essex, Esquier. Philip now my wife. Cecily late my wife. Certain Manors and lands to wife Philip for life, with these remainders :—(i.) the right heirs of my body ; (ii.) the heirs male of my brother Rauffe Josselyn ; (iii.) my cousin Rauffe Josselyn, son of John Josselyn late of Sheryng, and his heirs male ; (iv.) Philip and Geffrey, brothers of last named Rauffe, and their heirs male ; (v.) my right heirs. Prayers for souls of myself and of my wives, of Cecily and Phelip my children, of my father and mother, of Thomas and George Bradbury, of Robert Fitzherbert and Elizabeth his wife. Indenture dated 18 June 16 Henry VIII., made between (i.) me the said John, (ii.) Sir Geffrey Gate, K^t, upon the marriage of my son and heir Thomas, with Dorothy daughter of said Sir Geffrey. George Josselyn to have an annuity of cvj^s viij^d out of my manor of Hidehall, until he be preferred to a benefice of xx^m yearly. Thomas Bradbury, my brother-in-law, late citizen and alderman of London, gave the manor of Manewden in Essex to Jane late his wife, for life, remainder to my son Thomas Josselyn and his heirs, remainder to his cousin William Bradbury, son of his brother Robert Bradbury.

To be buried in the priory of Kings Hatfelde by late wife Cecily. Son Thomas now under xxiiij years. Anne Josselyn my daughter (spinster.) Jane my daughter and her husband. Costs and charges that I have borne for Cecily my late wife in suing for a special livery of her lands before our marriage "and otherwise for an hundred pounde sterlinge to John Fitzherbert for my said wife paide without lawe or conscience seying that she was first wedded to the sonne of the said John Fitzherbert having nothyng by him and afterward solde her ageyn to me for the said hunded pounde." John Tyrell, K^t, Humfrey Fitzherbert, William Bradbury and Sigesmond Coton, esq^{rs}, my feofees. Cousins George, Gabryell, and John Josselyn. My brother Gates. Sr Roger Wentworth, Knight, John his son and heir, and Anne his wife, my cousin. Exors, wife Phelip, Robert Norwiche, serjeant-at-law, Thomas Awdeley, Benjamyn Dygby, gent., and John Wiseman. My

I

master Sr John Veer, K^t, overseer. Witness : Sr Geffrey Gate, K^t, Guy Crayford, gent., Dame Joane Bradbury widow, Henry Susshe. Dated 12 July 17 Henry VIII. Proved 13 February 1525 by relict. Power reserved &c.

P.C.C. 3 Porch.

1526.

DAME ELIZABETH CLIFFORD late wife to Sir Robert Clyfford Knyght of Aspeden in the dioce of lincoln. To be buried by said Sir Robert in the church of Aspeden. Elizabeth, daughter to Thomas Clyfford, Esq., my son. My sister Anne Burton. Niece Elyanor Snowe, gentlewoman. Elizabeth daughter to Robert Barlee, gent. Elyano^r Eldergate. Prayers for my soul and for the souls of Sir Raufe Joslyn and Sir Robert Clyfford, Knights. To Thomas Stonar my teñt in Aspeden Street which Humfrey Griffen did dwell in, for his life, with remainder to my said son Thomas. Edward Mygar. X͡pofer Cheppe my godson. Residue of goods, with all manors, lands &c. to said son Thomas. Ex̃ors, son Thomas Clyfford and Thomas Stonar, Witness : Sir Robert Newman " parishe prest" Sir Georde Hoggesdon. William Snowe. Dated 1 May 1525. Proved 20 July 1526 by Thomas Clifford in person, and by Richard Felde, proctor to the other ex̃or.

P.C.C. 9 Porch.

1564.

SIR THOMAS JOSSELYN of Newehale Josselyn in the Countie of Essex, Knyghte. To be buried in the parish church of Sabridgworth, co. Herts., in the chancel. To my wife Dame Dorathe Josselyn "all my pearles and stones and all my Jewells—all my plate of siluer and siluer and gilt—and all my houshould stuff—at my manor c. mansion house of Newhalle Josselyn." John Gybbe, Thomas Perry, and John Ingolde stand seised of my manor of Highe Rothing and my lands in High Rothing, Gythorp Rothing, Kyngs Hatfelde and Canfeld or elsewhere in Essex, to the performance of my will as by a deed dated 30 September 4 Elizabeth. I will that my feoffees stand seised to the use of my said wife and of my son John Josselyn and the survivor of them, with remainder to the heirs male of my son Richarde Josselyn. Remainder to my son Thomas Josselyn and his heirs male. Remainder to heirs male of said John Josselyn. Remainder to my son Henrye Josselyn and his heirs male. Remainder to my son Edwarde Josselyn and his heirs male. Remainder to right heirs. To my son Richard my household stuff at Hide Hall, co. Herts. To my daughter Jane Kelton, wife of Richard Kelton gent. 100^l. Sr John Wentworth and wife. My son Glascok. Cousin Mathew Bradbury. My sister Dame Jane Wentworth. Son Henrye and Anne his wife. Wife Dorathe and son John, ex̃ors. Friends, George Hadley, Esq. and Roger Trigge, gent., overseers. Witness : John Spytty, Richard Choppin, Robert Wasket, John Gybb, Roger Trigge. Dated 1 October 4 Elizabeth. Adm̃on (with will annexed) 18 October 1564 to Dame Dorothy Josselyn the relict, the ex̃ors renouncing.

P.C.C. 28 Stevenson.

2

1582.

DAME DORATHEY JOSSELYN of Highe Roodinge in the Countie of Essex widowe, late the wife of Sᵣ Thomas Josselyn, Knighte, deceassed. To be buried next said husband in the church of Sabbesforde. To each of my sons "a ringe of golde." My daughter Jane Kelton. Humfrey Josselyn (minor), son to Humfrey Josselyn. Servant Richard Lucas. I make my brother, Sᵣ Henry Gate of Seamer, co. Ebor, Knight, my sole exor, paying my debts expressed in a schedule annexed to a deed indented made by me to my said brother, dated 7 July 18 Elizabeth. To Edwarde Josselyn, my son, the moiety of my remaining goods and to his daughter Marye Josselyn (minor) 20ˡ. Sᵣ William Cordell, Knight, to be overseer. Witness: Richarde Lucas, John Pickeringe, Hughe Glaue. Dated 10 June 1579. Admᵒⁿ (with will annexed) granted 14 February 1582 to Sᵣ Henry Gate, Kᵗ., who renounces exorship.

P.C.C. 10 *Rowe.*

1606.

THOMAS JOSLIN of Rocheford in the Countie of Essex, yeoman. To be buried in the church yard of Rochford. Land called Lytle Snares in Hockley, to the use of the poor of Rochford. To Edmond Thorneton, the elder, of Much Stanbridge. My kinsman Edmonde Thorneton of Shopland, John Freeborne, and Christopher Pake of Prittlewell, 40ˡ to the use of "the moste distressed and religious Ministers of the church of God." Mr. Culverwell of Much Stanbridge. Mr. Roger the elder, the preacher of Weathersfeild. Mr. Neagoose of Lee. Mr. Andrewes of Barlinge. Mr. Joslinge my kinsman, the preacher of Goodeaster. Mr. Catlyn of Bromfield. Mr. Dykes, a preacher in prison. Mr. Derrick. Ezechias and Samuel Lockin (minors) and their motherˡ My sister Elizabeth Sumner and her children. My sister Joane Lee, 20. by the hands of John Elliott of Litle Stambridge, no part going to her husband. Kinswomen, Jone Thorneaton, Lyddia Lee, and Rose Ellyott. My sister Phillis Gooddy. Wife's kinswoman, Margery Bachiler (a minor) 10ˡ. To the children of my brother Rafe Joslin of Roxwell, 150ˡ. To Henry Joslyn of Monesinge, my land called Thistledon's, (my wife's third excepted). Residue of houses and lands to wife Margaret for life. The remainder of a house in Rochford called Waterings, I give to William Taynetor and his heirs, remainder to James Nuttall, my wife's second son. The remainder of the residue of houses and lands I give to John, son of my brother John Joslynn the elder. I give my lease of the Wickhouse grounds in Childerditch and Westehornedon to Margaret my wife and John Joslin, son of my brother John Joslyn the younger, with remainder to the same John and his heirs, remainder to the youngest son of my brother John, the elder. My brother Rafe Joslin and Simon Joslyn shall be guardians to the said John in his minority. John Alyor. James Edgiott. Marie Eve of Rochford, and Thomas, Suzan, and Anne Eve, her children. My daughter-in-law Elizabeth Sams, daughter to Henry Sams late of Totham. My sons-in-law Edward Sams, Charles Nuttall, and James Nuttall.

3

Thomas, son of James Nuttal. The three children of Charles Nuttall. James and Marye, children to James Nuttall. To Jeffery Joslyn I give his debt to me. William Hudson of Rochford. My sister Bayllie's three younger children. Residue to wife Margarett, extrix. Witness: Thomas Burnett, Tobias Hudson, Thomas Woode. Dated 5 March 1604. Proved 12 December 1606 by relict and extrix.

P.C.C. 92 *Stafford.*

1627.

EDWARD JOCELINE. To son Henry Joceline, and to daughters Jane and Elizabeth Joceline, 50^l each. To my son Lovet, who married my daughter Anne Joceline, 40^l, so that he procure his wife a life-estate in the farm at Nutworth, where his father dwelleth. To my daughter Sydey, 30^l, to be bestowed on "some prettye house" to remain to her daughters. To William Sydey the younger, 5^l. To Wallgraue Sydey. To the children of my son-in-law Richard Stubbins, 60^l of the money my son Peter Gate oweth me, the remainder whereof I give to Joceline Gate, his son. To Mr. Wallis 5^l, he being my overseer. To my son Henrye, and daughters Jane and Elizabeth, my exors, all household stuff &c. they bestowing "a faire graue stone upon me with some Epitaph to shewe who I was and whence descended, vid^t the fourth sonne of Sr Thomas Joceline, K^{nt} of the Bath, and that I married Marye, the daughter and heire of one Lambe of Midlesex, by whom I hadd manye sonnes and daughters." My cousin Anthony Joceline oweth me 8^l, to be paid at his marriage. Witness: Richard Wallis, clerk, Jane Joceline, Eliz: Joceline. Undated. Proved 26 April 1627 by Henry Joceline. Power reserved &c.

P.C.C. 42 *Skynner.*

1632.

RALPH JOSSELYN of Roxwell in the County of Essex, yeoman. To wife Dorothy, a yearly rent of 20^l for life, she abiding with my sons Ralphe and Symon. My brother Symon Josselyn. I have given unto my eldest son John his full part of my estate, amounting to about 800^l. Raphe, son of said John. Mary and Anna my daughters. To my son Richard, 200^l for his portion, and in recompense of 15^l given him by will of my brother Thomas Josselyn, deceased. To my son Joseph Josselyn, 160^l. To son Nathaniell, 100^l. My daughter Elizabeth. Residue of goods to sons Ralph and Symon Josselyn, my exors. Son Nathaniell Josselyn, overseer. Witness: Ma: Bridges, William Rochell, William Smith, Cha: Smyth. Dated 3 September 1628. Proved 4 May 1632 by Ralph and Simon Joslin, the sons and exors.

P.C.C. 57 *Audley.*

1636.

THOMAS JOSSELIN, one of the secondaries in the Office of the Kings Ma^tis Remembrancer in the Court of Exchequer. If I die in London, to be buried "in the Chauncell of the Parrish Church of Greate St Bartholomewes where I dwell." If I die in the country, to be buried "in the church of Little Horkesley neere to my father." To wife Susanna Josselin the capital messuage wherein I dwell, with its lands in Little Horkesley, and a messuage and lands called Baldwynes &c. for life, with remainder to Thomas Josselin my son (a minor) and his heirs and assigns. Said wife, my cousin Edmund Saunder, esq̃, and my friend Mr. William Duckett, exõrs and trustees. Tenement in Lavenham, co. Suff. in tenure of Mary Josselin widow (my brother's late wife). My daughters Jane and Elizabeth (minors). My brother Phillip Josselin and his wife, and his brother-in-law Mr. William Witham. My brother John Josselin's heirs. My brother Francis Josselin. My son to be kept at school, at the university, and at the Inn of Court. Mary Light, my sister's daughter, hath since her mother's death been partly maintained by rents of teñts at Coggeshall. My brother Ancell, my said sister's former husband. Brother Lyte now living. Susanna and Frances Locke, my wife's daughters. Thomas Hide. Dame Phillip Carey, wife of Sir Ferdinando Carey, and her children. My sister Amyce and her children. My brother Amyce. Witness: Vincent Welly, Henrie Hamond, Tho: Hide. Dated 4 August 1635. Proved 26 April 1636 by exõrs.

P.C.C. 37 Pile.

1639.

SORRELL JOSLYN of Christ Church parish in London, bachelor. *Nuncupative will.* All goods to brothers and sisters equally. Witness: John Millward, Barbara Bott. Dated 9 May 1639. Admõn (with will) granted 16 May 1639 to Richard Joslyn the brother.

P.C.C. 95 Harvey.

1642.

JOHN JOSLIN of the parish of Slethians in the county of Cornwall, yeoman. Annis, wife of Henry Murton. John and Charity Murton. Kinsman John Tubb of St Allen, and his children. Kinsmen, Richard Smalley and Francis Smalley. Jane Smalley. Margaret Earle. James Lawry and his four brothers, and Johan Lawrie their mother. Henry Carverth the elder. Richard and Dorothie Harris. Phillis, the wife of William Lance. Residue to Henrie Bath, and James Bath his brother, of Slethians, my exõrs. Witness: Will: Knava, Edward Stephens, Wiħm Spurway. Dated 23 November 1640. Proved 14 May 1642 by exõrs.

P.C.C. 57 Cambell.

1645.

SYMON JOSLYN of Puckeridge in the parish of Braughing in the county of Hertford, draper. To son Thomas Joslyn the ware in my shop, he paying my debts, and 20ˡ to my father Markwell. To my four daughters, Elizabeth, Maria, Sarah, and Margaret Joslyn, the profit of my corn in Braughin, Standon, and Starford, at their ages of 18 years or marriage. My brother Thomas Joslyn of Chelmsford. To Anne Kendricke " her mothers Trunke and Bible and silver bodkin and silver thimble and my second great Kettle and box wᶜʰ was Margaretℓ." To Margaret Joslyn, my daughter, " her mothers Trunke." My son-in-law John Kendricke (under 21 years) and my daughter Joane Joslyn (under 18 years). My friend Thomas Mensant and my son-in-law Joseph Chunn and his wife. Dorothie, wife of John Churrie. Residue to son Thomas Joslyn, ex̄or. Witness: Thomas Measant, Dorothie Churrie. Dated 28 May 1645. Proved 21 July 1645 by ex̄or.

P.C.C. 90 Rivers.

1655.

SYMON JOCELINE of Easthaningfeild in the county of Essex, yeoman. To my eldest son Symon Joceline, my part of the messuage &c. called Boulingehatch in Roxwell and Newlandfee, with lands called Flax Hoppett, Willow Lease, Badhams, Asponfeild, Pearecrofte, &c., and so much of Moateshott whereof no use is limited by a certain deed of the division of the two parts of the said messuage &c. called Boulingehatch, made between Ralph Joceline of Roxwell, co. Essex, yeoman, Thomas Joceline of Barham, co. Suffolk, yeoman, and Rebecca his wife, and me the said Symon, of the one part; and Aron Benton and John Parey of London, gent., of the other part. I give my customary messuages and lands in Rettingdon to Peter Joceline. To my three daughters, Anna, Sarah, and Grace Joceline (minors), £100 each, over and above the sum of £50 which Peter Awecrofte, my late father-in-law (their grandfather), gave to my said three daughters and to my son Peter Joceline. Household stuff &c. given to my children by their grandfather and grandmother Awecroft. Residue to eldest son Symon, my ex̄or. My brothers, Nathaniell and Richard Joslyne, overseers. Witness: Thomas Luncher, George Solme. Dated 28 September 1649. Proved 6 February 1655 by ex̄or.

P.C.C. 54 Berkley.

1655.

SIMON JOSSLIN of Rayne in the county of Essex, yeoman. To my wife Ellin Josslin 5ˢ. To my son Simon Joslin my messuage &c. in Rayne called " Fortyes." To my son John Josslin my messuage wherein I dwell in Rayne Street. To my son Thomas 35ˡ. To my son Matthew 25ˡ. To my daughter Mary 15ˡ, and to my daughter Annis one shilling. To Mary and Sarah Maidwell 20ˢ each. Residue to sons Thomas and John, ex̄ors. Witness: Thomas Westley, Joseph Hills. Dated 28 July 1655. Proved 15 October 1655, by ex̄ors.

P.C.C. 384 Aylett.

HENRY JOCELINE of Okenton in the county of Cambridge. Joceline Gate, son of my sister Gate. Mary Dawkenᵱ, one of the daughters of my sister Gates. Elizabeth Dawkens and Peter Dawkens, and his twin brother, children of my goddaughter Dawkens. Humphry Downes, a grandchild of my sister Gates. Walgrave and William Siday, sons of my sister Siday. William Sidays two daughters by his first wife. Elizabeth Till, a daughter of my sister Siday, and her eldest daughter. Dorothy Stubing and Izabell Ward, daughters of my sister Martin. Edward Lovett son of my sister Lovett. Mary Siday, daughter of my sister Siday. Jonathan Mathewe of Okenton and Alice his wife. Robert Mathewe, my godson. John Smith of Okenton, and Thomas Smith, my godson. To my cousin Edward Ball, if living, " my Bookes of Martirs —and Hollinsheads Cronicles." Kinsman Mʳ Ratcliffe Todd, and Mʳˢ Ann his wife, and Mʳˢ Ann Todd his daughter. Kinswoman Mʳˢ Ann Highiam at Cowbridge. Friends, Mʳ Thomas Thompson the elder, and Mʳ Thomas Thompson the younger. Residue to sister Elizabeth Joceline, extrix. Kinsman Mʳ Waldegrave Siday, overseer, Witness : Jonathan Mathew, Robert Mathew, Thomas Waman. Dated 24 January 1653. Proved 11 June 1657 by extrix.

P.C.C. 216 Ruthen.

1657.

SIMON JOSSELIN of Burnham in the county of Essex, yeoman. To my daughter Sarah Josselin £40 at marriage or 21 years. To my wife Sarah Josselin, my freehold tent in Little Rayne, until my said daughter come to 21 years, when my wife shall enjoy only her thirds. My cousin Nathaniell Maydwell. The children of my sister Anne Bucknall. Matthew and Elizabeth, children of my brother Matthew Josselin. Residue to wife Sarah, my extrix. Friends, John Goulding and Thomas Stace, overseers. Witness : Edward Palmar, Daniel Stace. Dated 17 August 1657. Proved 23 November 1657 by extrix.

P.C.C. 365 Ruthen.

1657.

RALPH JOSSELIN of Cranham Hall in the county of Essex, yeoman. I give to my daughter Dorothy 100ˡ, owed me upon bond by Mʳ Ford, minister of Great Warely, she paying my daughter Grace 20ˡ. My nephew Ralph Jocelin, minister of Earl's Colne. Residue of goods &c. to daughter Elizabeth (unmarried). Said cousin Ralph, and my daughters Dorothy and Grace, exors. Witness: Richard Joslin, Ann Hampson. Dated 27 November 1656. Nuncupative Codicil dated 21 March 1656: I give 20ˡ in the hands of Captain Stracy to my daughter Grace, wife of Robert Johnson. Witness: Martyn Curtis, Ann Howard. *No Probate clause.* Proved between 23 and 29 December 1657.

P.C.C. 511 Ruthen.

JOHN JOSLIN, Citizen and Cutler of London. To my father Richard Joslin, and my mother-in-law Ursula his wife, 30ˡ. To my brother Richard Joslin 30ˡ, and to Mary Joslin, his daughter, by Anne his wife, 10ˡ. My brother Daniell Joslin, citizen and mason, and Rebecca his wife, and Elizabeth their daughter. My brother Edward Joslin. My brother Francis Joslin (minor). My sister Theoball Joslin (a minor). Elizabeth Overton of St. Margarets, Lothbury, spinster. My uncle Richard Playford of Sᵗ Olaves, Hart Street. Residue to brother Daniell Joslin, eẍor. Witness: James Smith, Henrie Playford. Dated 6 March 1657. Proved 15 April 1658 by eẍor.

P.C.C. 136 Wotton.

165$\frac{8}{9}$.

JOHN JOSHLYN of Royden in the county of Essex, yeoman. To my *son* Martha Joshlyn 30ˡ. To my son John Joshlyn 1ˢ. To wife Mary, 200ˡ now upon bond, with remainder to Ann Joshlyn my daughter. Residue to daughter Ann. Wife Mary, eẍtrix. Witness: Mary Bushee, Samuell Stracye. Dated 14 August 1658. Proved 31 January 165$\frac{8}{9}$ by relict and eẍtrix.

P.C.C. 24 Pell.

1662.

GILES JOSCELINE of Brabraham in the county of Cambridge, yeoman. To my son Arthur Josceline, all household implements and stock in Brabraham. My sons Francis and Edmond. "My best silver flaggon, and three silver spoones I give and bequeath vnto my sonne Giles," to whom I give my household stuff and stock in Linton. To my son Francis and his heirs all messuages lands and teñts in Little Abbington, Brabraham and Pampisford. To my son Arthur and his heirs my house and closes in Balsham. To my son Edmond and his heirs my free and customary messuages and lands in Depden, co. Essex, in occupation of Seamor. To my sons Francis and Edmond Joscelyne my freehold messuages and lands in Depden, in occupation of Beadle. Residue of messuages and lands to my sons Gyles and Arthur. To my son Richard, 5ˢ (he having had his portion). To my grandchild Richard Josceline, 10ˡ at 21 years. To my sons Francis and Edmond, 20ˡ each at 28 years. Residue to sons Gyles and Arthur, eẍors. Witness: Thomas Rickard, Robert Hacke, Edmond Joslin. Dated 17 September 1662. Proved 11 November 1662 by eẍors.

P.C.C. 144 Laud.

1668.

ELIZABETH JASLIN of Shadwell in the parish of Stebunheath, co. Mx., widow. To my daughter Hannah Woolward, wife of William Woolward, mariner, 60ˡ, which, at her death, shall be given to her children William and Elizabeth. Stephen North. Residue to Hannah Woolward and Thomas and Stephen Cockshutt. Said Hannah and Thomas, exͦrs. Son-in-law Woolward and friend Mͬ Anthony Knightsbridge, genᵗ, of Chensford overseers. Witness: Christopher Jackson, John Shott. Dated 21 November 1666. Proved 5 January 1668 by exͦrs.

P.C.C. 7 Coke.

1670.

JOHN JOSCELYNE of Fering in the county of Essex, esq̃. To my eldest son Nathaneel Joscelyne and his heirs, the messuage in Fering wherein I inhabit, with its free and copyhold lands. To my youngest son John Joscelyne, my messuage and lands in Layer Bretton. Certain messuages and lands near Sturmer, after my death descend to the heirs of Mary my late wife, begotten by me, and in default the fee simple is in me, and whereas my late father, myself, and my son Nathaneel had our education in Emanuel College in Cambridge, in case both my sons die without issue, I give the said messuages and lands to the Master and Fellows of the said College [for various purposes, amongst others, the augmentation of the Hebrew lectureship at Queen's College founded by testator's great uncle and godfather, John Joscelyne esq̃. Testator was born in Sabridgworth, where his cousin Sͬ Robert Joscelyne, Barᵗ, now dwells]. My chambers in Gray's Inn I give to my son Nathaneel. Cousin Sͬ Robert Joscelyne, my best friend Richard Harlakenden, esq̃, my kind brother-in-law Wͫ Pennoyer, esq̃, and my sister his wife, Hezekiah Haynes and John Eldred. Exͦrs to buy "Two dozen of Escutchions of the Armes of my Family and present them among my other friends." Mͬ Butcher, minister of Fering. Residue to son Nathaneel my exͦr. William Pennoyer overseer. Witness: John Cox. Dated 26 May 1668. Codicil dated 25 August 1670. Proved 21 November 1670 by exͦr. Admͦon *de bonis non* granted 19 February 1671 to Anne Joscelyne, relict and exͭrix of said exͦr, decᵈ.

P.C.C. 166 Penn.

1671.

NATHANIEL JOSCELYNE. "Had not I best aske my Father if I dye in this Sicknesse whether he will continue the payment of of my wifes portion and enjoyne my brother to buy the lands and receive the money and take the lands after her death." "If my wife be with child of a sonne, I give the lands in Sturmere and Feering to it and the heires males of its body and for want of such issue to my brother and the heires males of his body the rem^r to my right heires." If she be with a daughter, my brother shall pay the daughter 1000^l at 21 years or marriage. To Mr Henry Hatton 100^l and his bond for 80^l. To M^r Na: Ball 10^l. Mary Ram and Mary Allen. To the poor of Feering 3^l. "To the poore of *Kel* 40^s if buried there with care." Old Mr Seers. Mr Davison's bond is in my study at Grayes Inne. Residue to brother. My brother and wife exors. Father and Mr Hatton overseers. To my brother N: Baker a ring. Witness: Ed: Baker. Dated 15 December 1671. Proved 24 January 1671 by Amy the relict, John Joscelyne, the other exor, being deceased.

P.C.C. 4 Eure.

1671.

JOHN JOSCELYNE of Feering in the county of Essex, gent. To be buried near my father and brother. One hundred rings at the price of ten shillings each to be given at my funeral, whereof twenty to be given to the relations and friends of my sister Amy Joscelyn (widow of my late brother Nathaniell). If the said Amy be with child of a son, I give to the said son all my messuages lands and tents in Feereing, Layer Bretton, and elsewhere in Essex. In default of such son I give the premises to John, son of my uncle Edward Joscelyne of Sheilds, near Newcastle-on-Tyne. To said Amy Joscelyne 200^l, and the money left by her husband in his house (wherein I dwell) at the time of his last going to London, and I give her brother Nathaniell Baker 20^l. To my cousin Courtman 10^l. To my cousin Susan Ramsdale 5^l. Mr Angur of Copford, clerk. Mr Randall Croxon. Mr Butcher, vicar of Feering. Mr Tabor, vicar of Keluedon. Henry Hatton. George Andrewes and Dorcas his wife. Mr John Negus of Messing. Mary Ram. Samuel Euerit. John Portway. Mary Allen. Alice Portway. Nicholas Ravens. Mr John Porter and his wife and Nathaniel Porter their son. John, son of Mr Leppingwell of Church Hall. Poor of Feering and Keluedon To cousin John Eldred of Earls Colne, esq, 50^l, and to Margaret his wife, 20^l. Said John Eldred, esq, exor. Residue to said after-born son of my brother, if any, with rem^r in default to said cousin John Joscelyne. Witness: John Brockwell, John Argar, Will: Aylett. Dated 29 December 1671. Proved 14 February 1671 by exor.

P.C.C. 16 Eure.

1671.

HEZECHIAH JOSLIN of Copford in the county of Essex, clerk. To my wife Jane Joslin my copyhold estate in Good Easter for life, rem^r to my brother Richard Joslin of Much Lee and his heirs, he paying to my brother John Joslin 100^l, to Elizabeth my sister, wife of Lawrence Porter of Much Lees, 50^l, to my brother Thomas Joslin of Much Lees 50^l, to my sister Anne Beak 50^l. To my wife, the interest of 450^l in hands of Mr. Robert Burdett, merchant in Gravell Lane, near Algate. To my brother John Joslin, my house and lands in Bishshop-starford. To my brother Thomas, and my sister Anne Beake, 100^l each. My sister Mrs Boradell. Cousin Benjamin Dyer. Brother Richard Joslin of Much Lees, residuary legatee and exõr. Witness: He: Haynes, Benj: Rous, William Keame. Dated 24 April 1671. Codicil undated. Mrs Martha Boradell. Suzan King and her sister Martha. Witness: Benj: Rous, He: Haynes, William Keame. Proved 16 May 1671 by exõr.

P.C.C. 62 Duke.

———

1673.

ROBERT JOSELIN of Waltham Holycrosse in the county of Essex, " Inholder." All my sheep and corn I give to Sarah my wife. All the goods in my house, which were my mother's at the time of my last marriage, I will that my mother have again at her disposal. To my brother John Joselin of Enfield, 35^s. Kinsman John Robinson of Waltham, tanner, William, Elizabeth, Anne, and Mary Robinson, his brothers and sisters, and John, William, and Anne Robinson, his three children. Thomas Dickenson, son-in-law to Christopher Dickenson of of Waltham, shoe maker. John, son of John West of Waltham, coach-man. Mary Turner, daughter of John Turner of Waltham, ashman. Richard, son of Thomas Campe of Gallow Hill. Anne Robinson my sister, relict of Roskana Robinson. Residue to wife Sarah, exõtrix. Witness: John Jeve, William Cocke. Dated 16 March 1672. Proved 23 May 1673 by exõtrix.

P.C.C. 60 Pye.

———

1674.

JANE JOCELINE of Bishopp Starford in the county of Hertford, widow. To my sister Mrs Martha Borradale of Steeple Bumsted, co. Essex, 6^l yearly for life. Niece Mrs Mary Burdett. Cousin Nathan Burdett. Cousin An: Burdett. Cousins Robert, Benjamin, Jane, Leister, and Wright Burdett. Cousin Benjamin Dyer. Servant Susan King. Old servant Martha Chappell. Residue to nephew Benjamin Rous of Great Clacton, exõr. Witness: Tho: Leigh, Ralph Manister, Susanna King. Dated 9 August 1673. Proved 1 April 1674 by exõr.

P.C.C. 47 Bunce.

11

1692.

PHILLIP JOSSLING of the precinct of St Katherine's near the Tower of London, mariner, *being outward bound to sea.* My friend Richard Freind of the same precinct, victualler, to be universal legatee, atťy, and exõr. Witness: Thomas Hussey, Lawrance Stedwell, Tho : Cornelius. Dated 15 August 1688. Admõn (with will) granted 2 December 1692 to Nicholas Felton, exõr of Dorothy Freind, dec^d, who was, while she lived, exẽtrix of Richard Freind, dec^d.

P.C.C. 225 Fane.

1697.

WILLIAM JOSLING belonging to his Majesty's Ship Canterbury, mariner. Son John Josling of St Philip's in Bristoll, to be universal legatee, atťy, and exõr. Witness: B : Beaumount, Nathaniell Lea, George Amers. Dated 31 May 1695. Proved 21 June 1697 by exõr.

P.C.C. 120 Pyne.

1698.

CHRISTOPHER JOSLING of Wapping, mariner. Residue of estate to brother Henry Josling during his life, with rem^r to friend John Gill of Wapping, waterman, whom I make my atťy and exõr. Witness: George Fowler, Ralph Piggett, Sam : Wills, Juñ, scr̃ at Wapping New Stairs. Dated 23 October 1689. Proved 28 April 1698 by exõr.

P.C.C. 102 Wit.

1699.

ARTHUR JOSCELYNE of Little Abington in the county of Cambridge, genť. To Elizabeth my wife, my farm in Hinxton, in the tenure of Christopher Cooper, during her life, with rem^r to my grand-daughter Elizabeth Joscelyne and her heirs for ever, if she marry with her father's consent. To my said wife I give my house in Little Abington wherein I dwell, with the homestall and closes. To Anne my daughter-in-law, my silver tankard. Poor of Great and Little Abington and Brabram. Residue to son Arthur Joscelyne, esq̃, exõr. Friends John Lone, esq̃, and John Jeffery, genť, to determine any dispute about my estate. Witness: Eliz : Mayer, John Pierce, D : Mayer. Dated 28 November 1696. Proved 31 July 1699 by exõr.

P.C.C. 117 Pett.

12

JOHN JOSCELYN of Feering, in the county of Essex, gent. To be buried in the churchyard near my son John. I give all my lands in Feering, Inworth and Kelvedon, and in Sturmere, Wratting, Ketton and Steeple Bumpsteed, unto Martha my wife. And I give my copyhold farm called Atwells in Wethersfield to my said wife, whom I make my eẍtrix. I make my cousins Stephen Beckingham and Robert Rogers my overseers. Witnesses :—John Garrett : Abraham Campion : John Homan. Dated 10 October 1704.

Codicil :—I give to my wife "my Ship Alehouse" in Inworth. Dated 6 December 1704.

Proved 11 July 1705 by eẍtrix.

P.C.C. 117 Gee.

SIR ROBERT JOCELYN of Hide Hall, in the parish of Sabridgeworth, in the county of Hertford, Bart. To be buried in the parish church. To my daughter Jane Jocelyn 1500^l. To my son Edward Jocelyn 800^l. To my son Thomas Jocelyn an annuity of 40^l for his maintenance, the same being in no way liable to his debts. To my daughter Margaret Maurice 40^l yearly during her life, the same being in no way liable to the debts of her husband (Mr John Maurice). My daughter Sarah, wife of Mr Thomas Picard. To my wife Dame Jane Jocelyn "my Coach and one pair of my best Coachhorses." I will that my wife have the use of my furniture and plate if she keep house at Hide Hall. To my daughter Sarah Picard and my sons George and John Jocelyn a gold ring each. I make my son Strange Jocelyn my sole eẍor. Witnesses :—Edward Foyle : John Strange : Wm Strange. Dated 20 February 1699. Proved 10 February 1713, by Sir Strange Jocelyn, Bart., the eẍor.

P.C.C. 29 Aston.

JAMES JOSSELYN, the elder, of Little Horkesly, in the county of Essex, yeoman. I give to my eldest son James Josselyn my messuage called the Manor or Priory of Little Horkesly with the lands belonging, which I lately purchased of Christopher Whichcote of London, merchant. I give to my son Hugh Josselyn my messuage and lands, purchased of the said Christopher Whichcote, in Mount Bures and Worningford, he conveying to my son John Josselyn, at his full age, the copyhold messuage and lands purchased of my late wife's father Hugh Rice. I give to my son Thomas Josselyn my freehold and copyhold messuages and lands which I purchased of my brother William Josselyn (which were formerly in my father's occupation and are now in mine), and also my copyhold messuage and lands that late were my brother Thomas Josselyn's (deceased) in Great and Little Horkesly, paying to my sister Elizabeth Church, widow, 2^l 10^s yearly during her life, and 20^s yearly to Ann Balls my housekeeper, and also to his two sisters Rose and Elizabeth Josselyn 20^l each at full age or marriage. My daughter Anne Josselyn (minor). Residue to son James Josselyn my exŏr. I make Edward Husbands of Little Horkesly, esq., and Thomas Paris of Nayland in Suffolk, genṫ, my overseers. Witnesses :— Macklin Green: John Agas: Edward Gage. Dated 29 September 1712. Proved 20 June 1713 by the exŏr.

P.C.C. 137 Leeds.

1724

MARTHA JOSCELYN of Kelvedon, co. Essex, widow. To be buried in the churchyard of Feering near my husband. I give my freehold lands and teñts in Sturmer, Wratting, Ketting and Steeple Bumsted to Thomas Dunbar of Kelvedon, clerk, and Bezaleel Sherman of Kelvedon, surgeon, in trust for the benefit of my daughter Martha Tayspill of Colchester (now wife of Benjamin Tayspill, linen draper). I give my copyhold messuage, farm and lands, called Atwells in Wethersfield, to my grandson Thomas Angier. I give my moiety of a copyhold messuage, farm and lands, called Mildwells and Pepps in Tolleshunt Knights and Tollesbury, to my granddaughter Anne Tayspill and her heirs, with rem^r in tail to my grandchildren Martha and Thomas Tayspill. To my grandson Samuel Angier, who lately went beyond the seas, 80^l if he returns. Anne Stacy of London, widow. Stephen Beckingham of London, esq. Residue to said trustees in trust for my said daughter Martha. Daughter Martha Tayspill, exŭtrix. Witnesses:—C: Phelps: Mary Walford: Ro^b Jegon. Dated 3 March 1721.

Admŏn (with will annexed) granted 17 April 1724, to Thomas Dunbar, the exŭtrix renouncing.

P.C.C. 87 Bolton.

1725

SAMUEL JOSLYN of the parish of Stepney, co. Middlesex, mariner. Wife Mary Joslyn, universal legatee and exŭtrix. Witnesses:—Elizabeth Oxley: Elizabeth Stanton: Tho: Huett, attorney. Dated 10 March 1711. Proved 15 February 1725, by exŭtrix.

P.C.C. 27 Plymouth.

1725

ARTHUR JOSELYNE of Stapleford in the county of Cambridge, esq. I give my farm at Ellington, co. Hunts, to Arthur Joselyne my son, charged with an annuity of 30^l to Anne my wife. To my four daughters 5^l each for mourning. I give all my lands in Hinxston and

Ickleton, co. Cambridge, and in Chesterford magna, co. Essex, to my son Arthur Joselyne, charged with payment of 250ˡ each to my daughters Frances and Mary Joselyne at marriage or full age. To my daughter Jane 200ˡ at marriage or full age. My eldest daughter Elizabeth. My son to perform my covenants made with Roger Sizer, esq., upon his purchase of Abingdon Estate. I make my son Arthur my ex̄or, and I make my wife his guardian during his minority. If my wife marry I make my friends Roger Sizer, esq., Mr Richard Humberston of Elmdon in Essex, Mr Stephen Baseley of Hoeton, co. Hunts, Gregory Wade of Shelford parva, esq., and John Brown of Royston, guardians of my son. Witnesses :—Gre. Wale : George Godwin : Henry Fletcher. Dated 24 August 1714.

Codicil I. : 24 August 1714. Codicil II. : 13 August 1717. Codicil III. : 10 April 1718.

18 February 1725 appeared Thomas Lewington, genᵗ, to testify to handwriting of the codicils.

Proved 19 February 1725, by ex̄or.

P.C.C. 25 Plymouth.

Administrations.

1591. Ap: 23. ANNE JOSSELYN of Willingale Dooe, co. Essex, widow, deceased. Administration to Thomas Josselyn, the son.

1591. Ap: 30. HENRY JOSSELYN of Torellę Hall in Willingale Doe, co. Essex, esq., deceased. A. to Thomas Josselyn the son, of goods left unadministered by Anne Josselyn, the relict and ex̄trix, now also deceased. (Will registered *5 Rutland*).

161⅝. March 9. FRANCIS JOSELYN of Crundon Parke in Orset, co. Essex, deceased. A. to Anthony Joselyn, the brother.

1637. Nov: 4. JANE JOCELIN of Okington, co. Cambridge, spinster, deceased. A. to Henry Jocelin, the brother.

1638. Sep: 29. RALPH JOSCELINE of Rayne parva, co. Essex, deceased. A. to Anne Josceline, the relict.

1655. Nov: 28. MARY JOSSELYN of Sᵗ Swithin's, London Stone, spinster, deceased. A. to John Josselyn, the father.

165⁶⁄₇. Jan: 14. MARY JOSLING of Sᵗ Swithins, London Stone, spinster, deceased. A. to Elizabeth Ley, *alias* Josling (now wife of Timothy Lay) the sister, of goods unadministered by John Josling, the father, now also deceased.

1678. Nov: 8. JACOB JOSELIN of Redrith, co. Surrey, in the ship "Dyamond" at Plymouth, co. Devon, deceased. A. to Elizabeth Joselin, the relict.

———

168½. Mar: 6. FRANCIS JOSCELYNE of Ickleton, co. Cambridge, deceased. A. to Deborah Joscelyne, the relict.

———

1683. Ap: 17. ELIZABETH JOSCELINE of Ickleton, co. Cambridge, an infant, deceased. A. to Debora Josceline, widow, the mother.

———

1685. July 21. EDMUND JOSELYNE of Fulburne, co. Cambridge, deceased. A. to Grace Joselyne, the relict.

———

1691. Nov: 18. JOHN JOCELIN of Enfield, co. Middlesex, in the Mint in Southwark, deceased. A. to William Steere, a creditor. Margaret Jocelin, the relict, renounces.

———

170⁶⁄₇. Mar: 3. RICHARD JOSLING in the royal ship "Dolphin," bachelor, deceased. A. to Elizabeth Queenavalt, wife and attorney to Robert Queenavalt, now in the royal service in parts beyond sea, the heir.

———

1714. Ap: 27. HENRY JOSELING of Stepney, co. Middlesex, deceased. A. to Elizabeth Joseling, the relict.

———

1728. June 9. The Honourable GEORGE JOSCELYNE of Maidstone, co. Kent, esq., deceased. A. to Dame Catherine Twisden, *alias* Joselyne, widow, the relict.

———

1730. Dec: 19. The Honourable GEORGE JOCELYNE of Maidstone, co. Kent, esq., deceased. A. d. b. n. etc., to John Jocelyne, esq., an exōr of the will of Dame Catherine Twisden, *alias* Jocelyne, the relict and admīx, now also deceased.

The foregoing are notes of all the Wills and Administrations to persons of the name of Joscelyne to be found in the Prerogative Court of Canterbury from 1525 to 1730.—F. A. C.

Cole Family.

My Father, Nathaniel Cole, Died October 9th, 1762, and was Buried
October 13th, in St. Mary's Church Yard, Colchester.

My Wife's Father, Samuel Cole, Died February 8th, 1772, and was Buried
the 9th in Dedham Church Yard.

My Son, Thomas Cole, was born at Dedham, July 3rd, 1761, A Bout half
an ower after One O, Clock in the After Noon, and the pirsons then
present their where as under Written

    Mr. John Fox Juner, Man Midwife
    Mrs. Elizth Strutt, Senor
    Mrs. Mary Cutting
    Mrs. Mary Gretom
    My Maid, Marthy Kisser

My Daughter, Sarah Martha Cole, was born at Dedham, July 13th, 1763,
A Bout forty Minutes after Eight O, Clock in the Morning, and the
pirsons then present their where as under written

    Mr. John Fox Juner, Man Midwife
    Mrs. Strutt, Senor
    Mrs. Gretom Mason
    Mrs. Phillips
    My Maid, Mary Edwards

My Son, Samuel Cole, was born at Maningtree, Septmr 15th, 1764,
A Bout Fower O, Clock in the Morning, and the pirsons then
present their where as under Written

    Mr. John Fox Juner, Man Midwife
    Mrs. Sarah Surry
    Mrs. Mary Ponder
    My Maid, Easter Edwards

My Daughter, Elizabeth Cole, was born at Maningtree, Septmr 15th,
1765, A Bout Fower O, Clock in the Morning, and the pirsons then
present their where as under Written

    Mr. John Fox Juner, Man Midwife
    Mary Coney Nurse
    Mary Edwards
    Easter Edwards

My Second Daughter, Elizabeth Cole, was born at Maningtree, November
11th, 1767, Between Six & Seven O, Clock in the morning, and the
pirsons then present their where as under Written

    Mr. John Rogers, Man Midwife
    My Sister, Sarah Cole
    Mrs. Sarah Le Jander
    Sarah Church
    Easter Edwards

My Son, John Cole, was born at Maningtree, May 1st, 1770, A Bout five
O, Clock in the After Noon, and the pirsons then present their
where as under Written

    Mr. John Rogers, Man Midwife
    My Sister, Sarah Cole
    Mrs. Sarah Le Janders
    Hannah Wheeley

My Son, Edward Wright Cole, was born at Maningtree, July 25, 1771, A Bout Seven O, Clock at Night, and the pirsons then present their where as under Written

> Mr. John Rogers, Man Midwife
> My Sister, Sarah Cole
> Mrs. Sarah Le Janders
> Sarah Wheely
> Hannah Wheely

My Second Son, Samuel Cole, was born at Maningtree 15th day of April 1773, A Quarter before Eight in ye Morning & the pirsons then present where as under Written

> Mr. John Rogers, Man Midwife
> Mrs. Sizer
> My Sister, Sarah Cole
> Mrs. Le Janders
> Susan Janders

My Son, Samuel Cole, Died December 2nd, 1764, and was Buried in the Chappel Yard at Maningtree.

My Daughter, Elizabeth Cole, Died Novembr 2, 1765, and was Buried in the same Yard.

My Second Daughter, Elizabeth Cole, Died January 10th, 1768, and was Buried in the same Yard.

My Daughter, Sarah Martha Cole, Died March 19th, 1768, and was Buried in the Chappel Yard at Maningtree.

My Son, John Cole, Died June 2nd, 1770, and was Buried in the Chappel Yard at Maningtree.

My Brother, Denney Cole, Died September 7th, 1767, and was Buried in the Chappel Yard at Maningtree.

> *From a Testament by William Burkitt, M.A., late Vicar of Dedham, Essex, dated 1765, in the possession of Thomas Springar Cole of Toronto, Canada.—F. A. C.*

Gall Family.

To all and singuler as well Nobles and Gentills as others to Whome these presentọ shall come Robert Cooke Esquire alias Clarencieulx principall Herauld and Kynge of Armes of the South East and Weast partes of this Realme of England from the Ryuer of Trent southward sendith greetinge in oure Lord God euerlastinge. Wher as auncyently from the begininge the valiant and vertuous actes of excellent Persons haue ben comendid vnto the world wth sondry monumentọ and Remembrancis of their good Deseartes Emongest the which the chiefest and most vsuall hathe ben the bearinge of Signes and Tokens in Shieldes called Armes which are non other then demonstracions of Prowes and valoir diuersely distributed according to the Quallityes and deseartes of the persons: Which Order as it was prudently deuysed in the begininge to stirre and kindle the hartes of men to the ymitacõn of vertue and noblenes: Euen so hathe the same ben and yeat is continually obserued to thentent that suche as haue don comẽendable seruice to their Prince or Contry ether in warre or peace maye bothe receaue due honor in their Lyeues and allso deryue the same successieuelly to their posteritye for euer. And beinge required of Robert Gall of London gentleman to make searche in the Regesters and Recordes of myne Office for the auncient Armes belonginge to that name and Famyly Wherof he is descendid: Wheruppon I haue made searche accordingly and do fynde the sayde Robert Gall to be the sonne and heire of Robert Gall of weneston in the countye of Suffolke gentleman, And of Mary his wyffe doughter and Coheire of Richard Marshall of Dunstable in the Countye of Buckingham gentleman: So that fyndinge the true and perfecte Descent, I could not with oute his great preiudice assigne vnto him any other Armes then those which are lyneally descendyd to him from his auncestors. That is to saye, Quarterly in the first for Gall, asur a Fesse siluer fretty of the fyeld, In the second for Marshall, sables thre battayll Axes gould, a Canton ermyns, In the third for Shelford, gold, a Cheueron asur betwene thre Trayfoiles gules, In the forth for Roderham, siluer a Fesse gules betwene thre Lozenges sables. And for that I fynde no Creast vnto the same as comonly to all auncient Armes there belongith none, I the sayd Clarencieulx Kynge of Armes By power and aucthorytie to my Office annexed and granted by Lr̃es Pattentẹ vnder the great Seale of England haue assigned geuen and granted to these his auncyent Armes the Creast herafter followinge. Vidz̃t, vppon the healme on a Wreath, siluer and asur, a Lyon seant siluer with a Crowne on his head, houldinge in his fore foote a battayll Axe gould, manteled gules, dobled siluer, as more playnly aperith depicted in the margent. To haue and houlde the sayde Armes and Creast vnto and for the sayd Robert Gall gentleman, and to his posteritye and to all the posteritie of Robert Gall his father with their differencis, And he and they the same to vse, beare and shew forthe in Shield, Cote, Armor or otherwayse at his and their Liberty and pleasure, with oute Impediment, Lett, or Interuption of any person or persons. In witnes wherof I the sayde Clarencieulx Kinge of Armes, haue signed these presentẹ with my hande, and haue sett herunto the Seale of myne Office the vjᵗʰ daye of June Anno Doñi 1576, and in the xxiiᵗʰ yeare of the Raigne of oure Soueraigne Lady by the Grace of God, of England Fraunce and Ireland Queene Defendres of the Faythe xc̃.

From the original Grant in my possession.—F. A. C.

Gilson Family.

Thomas Gilson, Bradley, Suffolk.

Thos Gilson Marred to Eleanor Woollard the 19 Day Dec 1799 and Eleanor Was Born 25 day of January 1777.

John Gilson Son to Thos & E. Gilson was born Sep 11th 1800 on Thusday Morning 4 Minets after 4 Oclock.

Thos Gilson Son to Thos Gilson and Eleanor his Wife was born the 5 of June ½ Parst 12 in the Morning 1802.

Alenton Gilson Son to Thos Gilson and Eleanor his Wife January 21 1804 ¼ after 11 Forenoon.

Ditto Wm Gilson Born April the 10th 1806 which Died in the Innfencey the 19 day April 1806.

Zadok Gilson Son to Thos Gilson and Eleanor his Wife was Born August 17th 1807 Ten Minets after Seven Oclock in ye Morning.

Thomas Gilson the son of Henry Gilson and Mary His Wife was Born the 20th Day of January 1733.

Henry Gilson the Son of Henry Gilson and Mary his Wife was Born March 28 Ano Dom 1736.

George Gilson the Son of Henry Gilson and Mary his Wife was Born the 9th Day of November 1739.

Ann Gilson the Daughter of Thos Gilson and Ann his Wife was Born the 21st Day of Febuary in the year 1761.

Mary Gilson the Daughter of Thos Gilson and Ann his Wife was Born the 14 Day of October in ye year Ano Dom 1762.

Hannah Gilson the Daughter of Thos Gilson and Ann his Wife was Born the 10th Day of Febuary Ano Dom 1764.

Sarah Gillson the Daughter of Thomus Gillson and Ann his Wife was Born the 21 of June 1766.

Alice Daughter of George Gilson and Alice his Wife was Born the 31st Day of July 1765.

Beatar Daughter of George Gilson And alice his wife was Born the 5 Day of may 1767. George Gilson The son of George Gilson and and alice his wif was Born The 24 of october 1769.

Mary Gilson the Daughter of George Gilson and alice his wife was Born the 29 of march 1772.

Rebekah the Daughter of George Gilson and alice his wife was Born the 26 day of Fabruary 1774.

Ann Gilson The Daughter of Georg Gilson And alice his wife was born The 18 day Augst 1778 And Babtised the 23.

Henry . . .
His wi . . .
Thomu . . .
Ann . . . .
Alice Gilson the . . .
and ann His . . .
of november . . .   *Leaf torn.*
December . . . .
Janu . . . . . .
Rebekah . . . .
And ann . . . .
Babtised th . . . . .
Fuller Will . . . . .

From a volume containing a Book of Common Prayer, dated 1761, and a Bible dated 1763, in my possession. On the title-page to the Bible is written "Mary Ann Denham, August 9th 1817."—F. A. C.

Felixstowe, Suffolk.

HERE LIETH INTERED THE BODY
OF JOHN SAWER WHO DEPARTED
THIS LIFE FEB. THE 12 : 1750 AGED
67 YEARS.
ALSO JANE HIS WIFE WHO DEPARTED
THIS LIFE NOVEMBER THE 14 : 1755
AGED 76 YEARS.

*On an altar tomb of brick with a stone top,
south of the chancel.*

———

HERE RESTETH THE BODY OF
ELIZABETH HYNDES
WHO DEPARTED THIS LIFE
JULY THE 17TH 1756 AGED 37
YEARS.

On a headstone, south of the chancel.

———

IN MEMORY OF
JOSEPH BUGG
WHO DIED YE 24TH OF NOVBR
1776
AGED 78 YEARS.

On a headstone, south of the chancel.

———

IN MEMORY OF
MARY THE WIFE OF
JOSEPH BUGG
WHO DIED
THE 30TH OF JULY 1782
AGED 54 YEARS.

On a headstone, south of the chancel.

———

IN THIS GRAVE
ARE DEPOSITED THE REMAINS
OF
SIR SAML BRUDENELL FLUDYER
BART.
WHO DIED 17 OF FEBRUARY
1833
AGED 73 YEARS.

*On an upright stone at the head of a coffin-shaped
monument, south of the chancel.*

IN THE GRAVE
ARE DEPOSITED THE REMAINS
OF
MARIA THE WIFE OF
SIR SAM^L BRUDENELL FLUDYER
BART.
WHO DIED 23RD OF NOVEMBER
1818
AGED 52 YEARS.

On an upright stone at the head of a coffin-shaped
monument, south of the chancel.

IN MEMORY OF
MARY THE WIFE OF
JOHN PAINE WHO
DIED THE 24ST JUNE 1764
AGED 32 YEARS.

On a headstone, west of the south transept.

SACRED TO THE MEMORY OF JOHN PIPE
WHO DEPARTED THIS LIFE JULY 28, 1839
AGED 66 YEARS.
ALSO OF FRANCES HIS WIFE
WHO DEPARTED THIS LIFE MAY 30, 1861
AGED 75 YEARS.

On a stone monument, east of the chancel.

SACRED TO THE MEMORY OF
CHARLOTTE ANNA WIFE OF JOHN WROOTS PIPE
WHO DIED 11TH SEPTEMBER 1854
AGED 31 YEARS.
ALSO OF HENRY INFANT SON OF THE ABOVE
WHO DIED 5TH SEPTEMBER 1850.

On a stone monument, east of the chancel.

IN REMEMBRANCE OF
WILLIAM WOODGATE
BORN AT RAYDON IN THIS COUNTY
DIED NOVEMBER 25TH 1883
AGED 84 YEARS.
ALSO OF
SARAH HIS WIFE
WHO DIED APRIL. 22ND 1885.
AGED 81 YEARS.

On a granite monument, east of the chancel.

OF YOUR CHARITY PRAY FOR THE SOUL OF
GEORGE DARELL SHEE
RECORDER OF HYTHE, KENT
WHO DIED AT FELIXSTOWE DECEMBER 15: 1894
AGED 51 YEARS.
R. I. P.

On a monument, south-east of the chancel.

————

IN LOVING MEMORY
OF
HENRY GEORGE QUILTER
WHO DIED NOVEMBER 23RD 1893
IN HIS 70TH YEAR.

On a cross of white marble, south-east of the chancel.

————

IN LOVING MEMORY OF
HENRY JERVIS WHITE-JERVIS
COL. ROYAL ARTILLERY
DIED SEPTEMBER 22, 1881, AGED 56 YEARS.
ETHEL ROSE JERVIS WHITE-JERVIS
BORN AUGUST 20TH 1862.
DIED MAY 11TH 1886.

*On a granite cross in the north-east corner
of the churchyard.*

————

WALTER WADE
ACCIDENTALLY DROWNED AT FELIXSTOW
5 SEPTEMBER 1869.

*On a stone cross in the north-east corner
of the churchyard.*

————

IN
LOVING MEMORY
OF
HYNMAN ALLENBY
BORN AUGUST 25, 1821.
DIED FEB. 20, 1878.

*On a granite headstone in the north-east
corner of the churchyard.*

23

IN MEMORY OF
HENRY BERNARD
INFANT SON OF
ARTHUR & ALICE
HEBDEN
DIED MAY 8TH 1868.

*On a granite headstone in the north-east
corner of the churchyard.*

————

IN MEMORY OF
SIR JOHN SPENSER LOGIN
WHO DIED HERE OCTOBER 18, 1863
AGED 53.
ERECTED BY THE MAHARAJAH DULEEP SINGH
HIS AFFECTIONATE WARD
IN GRATEFUL REMEMBRANCE OF THE TENDER CARE WITH
WHICH HE TRAINED HIM UP IN THE SIMPLE FAITH OF OUR
LORD AND SAVIOUR JESUS CHRIST.
IN MEMORY
OF
SIR JOHN SPENSER LOGIN
WHO DIED AT FELIXSTOWE
ON THE 18TH OCT. 1863
IN THE 54TH YEAR
OF HIS AGE.
THIS MONUMENT IS ERECTED
BY HIS AFFECTIONATE FRIEND AND WARD
THE MAHARAJAH DULEEP SINGH
IN GRATEFUL REMEMBRANCE
OF THE TENDER CARE
AND SOLICITUDE WITH WHICH
SIR JOHN LOGIN
WATCHED OVER HIS EARLY YEARS
TRAINING HIM UP IN THE PURE
AND SIMPLE FAITH OF OUR LORD AND SAVIOUR
JESUS CHRIST.
EDWARD WILLIAM SPENCER LOGIN
INDIAN IMPERIAL FINANCE
ELDEST SON OF SIR J. S. AND LADY LOGIN
DIED AT SEA OFF GALLE
DECEMBER 16, 1876
AGED 33.

*On a large monument of marble and granite, north-east
of the chancel.*

Copied 9th September, 1895.—F. A. C.

Alderton, Suffolk.

IN THE CHURCH.

IN MEMORY OF ELEANOR DOUGLAS NORTON
WIFE OF THE REVEREND WILLIAM ADDINGTON NORTON, M.A.
RECTOR OF THIS PARISH
AND GRANDAUGHTER AND HEIRESS AT LAW OF JOHN FOX
OF PARLIAMENT STREET, WESTMINSTER
AND OF GREAT DOODS, REIGATE, IN THE COUNTY OF SURREY ESQUIRE
WHO DIED ON THE EIGHTH DAY OF DECEMBER
IN THE YEAR OF OUR LORD 1834 AGED 38 YEARS.
ALSO OF THREE OF THEIR CHILDREN
WILLIAM DOUGLAS NORTON
WHO DIED APRIL 27TH 1827 AGED THREE YEARS
AND AUGUSTUS ADDINGTON AND CATHARINE NORTON
WHO DIED IN INFANCY.

On a white marble tablet on the north wall.

TO THE MEMORY
OF
THE REVD ROBERT BIGGS, A.B.
46 YEARS RECTOR OF THIS PARISH
AND LATE VICAR OF BAWDSEY.
HE WAS NOT DISTINGUISHED BY
HIS ACTIVITY
OR
LITERARY ABILITIES
BUT HE WAS
WHAT IS MORE TRULY VALUABLE
AN HONEST MAN.
HE DEPARTED THIS LIFE 8TH OCTR 1769
AGED 72 YEARS.
THIS MONUMENT WAS ERECTED BY HIS TWO EXECUTORS
THOMAS CUDDON, ONE OF THE MASTERS IN ORDINARY OF THE
HIGH COURT OF CHANCERY OF GREAT BRITAIN
AND
PETER MABER ESQR BOTH OF THIS COUNTY.

On a white marble tablet on the north wall.

25

IN
MEMORY OF
SAMUEL GROSS
LATE OF PETISTREE
AND FORMERLY OF THIS PARISH
WHO DIED JUNE 24TH 1836
AGED 72 YEARS.
ALSO OF ANN HIS WIFE
WHO DIED JANUARY 3RD 1815 AGED 59 YEARS.
ALSO OF THEIR SON
SAMUEL CHILTON GROSS
OF THIS PARISH
WHO DIED MARCH 17TH 1844 AGED 47 YEARS.
ALSO OF
ANNA ELIZA EMILY
INFANT DAUGHTER OF
WOOLNOUGH AND ANNE ELIZA MARIA GROSS
(AND GRAND-DAUGHTER OF
SAMUEL CHILTON GROSS)
WHO DIED DECEMBER 24TH 1848.
ALSO OF
ANN, RELICT OF SAMUEL CHILTON GROSS
AND SECOND DAUGHTER OF
JOHN WOOLNOUGH
LATE OF WOODBRIDGE AND FORMERLY OF BOYTON
SHE DIED AUGUST 5TH 1881 AGED 80 YEARS.

On a stone monument let into the north wall.

———

IN A VAULT
UNDER THIS MONUMENT
ARE DEPOSITED THE REMAINS OF
JOHN PYTCHES ESQ^{R}
WHO DIED OCTOBER THE 28TH 1803
AGED 66.
MARY HIS WIFE
DIED OCT^{R} 16TH 1827
AGED 85.
ELIZABETH PYTCHES
DIED NOV^{R} 23RD 1823.

On a monument of white marble on the north wall.

26

IN MEMORY OF
THURSTON WHYMPER ESQ^R
YOUNGEST SON OF
M^R THO: WHYMPER LATE OF GLEVERING HALL
IN THIS COUNTY.
WHO DIED AT WOODBRIDGE AUG^T 21ST 1794 AGED 41 YEARS.
AND OF HIS WIFE
M^RS ELIZABETH WHYMPER
WHO DIED APRIL 28TH 1823, AGED 63 YEARS.
THEIR REMAINS REST WITHIN THE STEEPLE.

On a marble tablet on the north side of the church.

IN THE CHURCHYARD.

WITHIN THE WALLS
OF THE CHANCEL LIETH THE
BODIES OF
ROBERT HOWARD
WHO DIED SEPT. 16, 1807
AGED 66 YEARS.
ALSO ANN HIS WIFE
WHO DIED JULY 16, 1783
AGED 44 YEARS.
ALSO SARAH
HIS SECOND WIFE
WHO DIED APRIL 15, 1810
AGED 54 YEARS.
TO THE MEMORY OF
JOHN DENNINGTON LEACH
WHO DIED JUNE 20TH 1859
AGED 74 YEARS.
TO THE MEMORY OF
SOPHIA BEDWELL LEACH
WHO DIED NOVEMBER 29TH 1867
AGED 81 YEARS.
SARAH
DAUGHTER OF JOHN
DENNINGTON & SOPHIA
BEDWELL LEACH
DIED OCTOBER 27, 1830
AGED 18 YEARS.
HOWARD JOHN
SON OF JOHN DENNINGTON
AND SOPHIA BEDWELL LEACH
LOST AT SEA
DECEMBER 24, 1836
AGED 22 YEARS.

On a stone monument, east of the church.

27

HERE LIETH THE BODY OF ANNA
THE WIFE OF JOHN WOOLNOUGH
OF THIS PARISH AND DAUGHTER OF
JONATHAN QUINTIN OF IPSWICH GEN[T]
HE DEPARTED THIS LIFE
THE 3[D] OF OCTOB: 1741.
AGED 30 YEARS.
AND ALSO THE BODIES OF
QUINTIN, JOHN, DEBORAH AND JOHN
THE CHILDREN OF THE SAID
JOHN AND ANNA WOOLNOUGH
AND ALSO TO THE MEMORY OF
JOHN WOOLNOUGH GENT.
OF THIS PARISH WHO WAS
BURIED THE 22ND OF NOV[R] 1768
AGED 74 YEARS.

On an altar tomb, east of the chancel.

HERE RESTETH IN HOPES
OF A JOYFULL RESURECTION
THE BODY OF JN[O] WOOLNOUGH
OF THIS PARRISH WHO DEPARTED
THIS LIFE THE 27: OF AUGUST
1728 AGED 59 YEARS.
HE WAS V: SON OF ROBART
WOOLNOUGH OF DENTON
IN NORFOLK
AND OF FRANCES THE WIFE OF
THE SAID JOHN WOOLNOUGH
WHO DEPARTED THIS LIFE
THE 30TH MARCH 1744
AGED 73 YEARS.

On an altar tomb of brick with a stone top, east of the chancel.

SACRED
TO THE MEMORY OF
SARAH BREDELL RODWELL
THE BELOVED WIFE OF
JOSHUA RODWELL
OF ALDERTON HALL IN THIS COUNTY
WHO DEPARTED THIS LIFE
SEPTEMBER 28TH 1853
AGED 57 YEARS.
ALSO OF
JOSHUA RODWELL
THE BELOVED HUSBAND OF THE ABOVE
WHO DEPARTED THIS LIFE
MAY 10TH 1867
AGED 79 YEARS.
ALSO OF
MARY JANE RODWELL
SECOND DAUGHTER OF THE ABOVE
WHO DIED AT WALTON, SUFFOLK
20TH FEBRUARY 1882
AGED 59 YEARS.

On a large stone monument near the south door.

SACRED
TO THE MEMORY OF
JOHN WOOLNOUGH ESQUIRE
LATE OF WOODBRIDGE
AND FORMERLY OF BOYTON
WHO LIVED HIGHLY RESPECTED
THROUGHOUT A LONG AND
HONOURABLE LIFE AND DIED
29TH DECEMBER 1833 DEEPLY
LAMENTED, IN THE 78 YEAR
OF HIS AGE.
ALSO OF
LOUISA HIS WIFE
WHO DIED 16TH MARCH 1851
IN THE 82ND YEAR
OF HER AGE.
ALSO OF
MARY REBECCA
ELDEST DAUGHTER OF
SAML CHILTON AND MARY GROSS
OF BAWDSEY
BORN DEC: 11, 1857 DIED FEB 20, 1875.
AND GREAT GRANDAUGHTER
OF THE ABOVE

On an altar tomb of stone, east of the chancel.

HERE RESTETH IN HOPES OF A
JOYFULL RESURRECTION THE BODY OF
SAMUEL VERTUE
OF THIS PARISH WHO DEPARTED THIS
LIFE JULY THE 11TH 1768
AGED 47 YEARS.

On a flat stone, north-east of the chancel.

Copied 12th September 1895.—F. A. C.

Bawdsey, Suffolk.

IN THE CHURCH.

ERECTED IN LOVING MEMORY OF
EDWARD CAVELL
OF BAWDSEY HALL
BORN 1802, DIED 1867.
ALSO OF
ANNE (BALDRY) CAVELL HIS WIFE
BORN 1814, DIED 1879.
BY THEIR AFFECTIONATE CHILDREN.

On a marble tablet on the north wall of the church.

KATHARINE MARY JOSEPHINE
TIGHE GREGORY
BURIED HERE
27 FEB: 1864.

On a flat stone in the aisle.

IN MEMORIAM.
KATHARINE MARY JOSEPHINE
TIGHE GREGORY
NÉE STEWART
LAST REPRESENTATIVE OF THE STEWART
OF BALLY-WILLAN AND BALLY-AUGHRIM
DESCENDANTS OF ALEXANDER 6TH LORD HIGH STEWART OF SCOTLAND A.D. 1273
WIFE OF THE VICAR OF THIS PARISH
DIED 20 FEB. 1864.
PHILIPP. IV. 8.

On a marble monument on the south wall of the church.

IN THE CHURCHYARD.

IN MEMORY OF
JOHN HARPER
LATE OF THIS PARISH
OB. 15 JUNE 1748
ÆT: 33.
ALSO ELIZ: HIS RELICT, LATE WIFE
OF JOHN BARTHORP
OF HOLLESLY
OB: 10 JAN: 1786.
ÆT: 63.
AND JOHN HARPER
THEIR ELDEST SON LATE OF
HASKETON OB: 4: MARCH 1775
ÆT: 30.

On an altar tomb of brick with a stone top, south of the tower.

————

SACRED
TO THE MEMORY OF
SAMUEL BURROWS
WHO DIED NOV: 7TH 1857
AGED 65 YEARS.

On an upright stone at the head of a brick tomb, north of the church.

————

IN MEMORY OF
JOSHUA BRYANT, GENT.,
(OF THIS PARISH)
WHO DIED 9TH SEP. 1853
AGED 57 YEARS.
ALSO
OF MARY, WIFE OF THOMAS EASTERSON
(RELICT OF THE ABOVE NAMED JOSHUA BRYANT)
WHO DIED NOV: 1ST 1858.
IN THE 49TH YEAR OF HER AGE.

On an altar tomb surrounded by iron railings, west of the tower.

31

IN
MEMORY OF
JOSHUA, SON OF
JOSHUA & MARY BRYANT
WHO DIED 28TH APRIL 1847
IN HIS 8TH YEAR.

On a headstone, near the last.

———

TO THE MEMORY OF CORRY CAVELL
LATE OF THIS PARISH GENTN
WHO DEPARTED THIS LIFE UPON THE 28TH DAY OF JANRY 1828
AGED 81 YEARS
ALSO OF MARY HIS WIDOW WHO DEPARTED THIS LIFE
UPON THE 29TH DAY OF DECR 1830
AGED 71 YEARS.
TO THE MEMORY OF
CORRY CAVELL
ELDEST SON OF CORRY & MARY CAVELL
WHO DEPARTED THIS LIFE
UPON THE 18TH DAY OF JUNE 1829
AGED 41 YEARS.
AT THE
FOOT ARE
THE REMAINS OF
ROBT & CHAS
TWO OTHER SONS
WHO DIED ROBT UPON
THE 8 FEB. 1795
AGED 3 MONTHS
CHAS UPON THE
16 SEP. 1803
AGED 10 YEARS.

On an altar tomb surrounded by iron railings, east of the chancel.

———

IN
MEMORY OF
EDWARD CAVELL
OF BAWDSEY HALL
WHO DIED JULY 3RD 1867 AGED 65.
ALSO OF ANNE HIS WIFE
WHO DIED JANUARY 31ST 1879 AGED 65.
EDWARD ERNEST ELDEST CHILD OF
EDWARD CHARLES AND EDITH CAVELL
DIED 5TH JULY 1876 AGED 8 WEEKS.

On a stone monument, south of the last.

32

TO THE MEMORY OF
JOHN JEAFFRESON OF THIS PARISH GEN[T]
WHO DYED AUGUST THE 6TH 1759 AGED 57.
ELIZABETH HIS WIFE WHO DYED
AUGUST THE 29TH 1759 AGED 62.
AND THEIR CHILDREN
ANNE LATE WIFE OF M[R] JOHN BARTHORP
OF ALDERTON WHO DYED FEBRUARY THE 2[D] 1760
AGED 29.
AND JOHN WHO DYED MARCH THE 16TH 1760
AGED 27.
IN DUTY, GRATITUDE & AFFECTION
TO KIND & INDULGENT PARENTS
TO A PRUDENT & TENDER WIFE
AND TO A DESERVEDLY BELOVED BROTHER
THIS MARBLE IS DEDICATED

*On an altar tomb of brick with a stone top,
on the south of the chancel.*

HERE LIETH THE BODY OF
ROBART DALLINGER
DEPARTED THIS LIFE THE 23
DAY OF DECEMBER 1722
AGED 40 YEARS AND ALSO
SARAH THE DAUGHTER OF
YE SAID ROB[T] DALLINGER
WHO DEPARTED THIS LIFE THE
1 DAY OF JANUARY 1722
AGED 12 YEARS.

On an altar tomb of brick with a stone top.

33

THIS TOMB STONE WAS RAISED
BY J. BRAND OF SUTTON
OVER THE BODY OF
A. M. E. SPENCER
WHO TO HIS GREAT SORROW
DEPARTED THIS LIFE
JANUARY 24TH 1829
AGED 24 YEARS.
IF ANY PERSONS TAKE THE TROUBLE
OF COMING INTO THIS NEIGHBOURHOOD
TO INQUIRE ABOUT ME
MERELY SAY THEY MAY FIND ME
IN BAWDSEY CHURCHYARD.

*An altar tomb of brick with a stone top surrounded by iron
railings, on the north side of churchyard.*

———————

MARGARET
TICHE-GREGORY
NÉE GARROD
WIFE OF THE REV. A. TIGHE-GREGORY
VICAR OF BAWDSEY.
BY BIRTH "LOW" AS THE BLESSED VIRGIN,
BY INTELLIGENCE, EDUCATION, MARRIAGE "RAISED"
IN THE ESTIMATE OF SOCIETY
BY EVERY WOMANLY GRACE & EVERY CHRISTIAN VIRTUE
"LITTLE LOWER THAN THE ANGELS."
AGE 33, APRIL 8, 1877.

On a headstone near the vicarage grounds.

Copied 12th September 1895.—F. A. C.

———————

Walton, co. Suffolk.

IN LOVING MEMORY OF
CHARLES HARWICK MARRIOTT
FOR TEN YEARS
VICAR OF WALTON AND FELIXSTOWE
BORN JAN. 13, 1815, DIED JAN. 11, 1893.
IN LOVING MEMORY OF
MARY ANN PALMER
WIFE OF THE
REV. C. HARWICK MARRIOTT
WHO ENTERED INTO REST
JAN. 5, 1890 AGED 54.

On a marble cross, south of the chancel.

Copied 13 September 1895.—F. A. C.

Admissions to Manors in Redenhall & Denton, co. Norfolk.

Manor of Alburgh Rectory. Special Court Baron of the Rev. Stair Fax Stillingfleet, rector, held 30 May 1748, before Daniel Sayer, steward. Admission of Anthony Freston of the parish of St Cross, als St George, als Sandcroft, in South Elmham, co. Suffolk, yeoman, on the surrender of Thomas Stubbs, clerk, he being cousin and next heir of Sarah Flowerdew, deceased.

Manor of Alburgh Rectory. General Court Baron held 5 February 1764, before Daniel Sayer, steward. Admission of Anthony Freston, an infant of the age of six years or thereabouts, eldest son and next heir of Anthony Freston, tenant of the said manor, who died since the last Court.

Manor of Denton Rectory. General Court Baron of the Rev. George Sandby, M.A., rector, held 12 November 1751, before Daniel Sayer, steward. Admission of John Van Kamp of Bungay, co. Suffolk, on the surrender of Elizabeth Postlethwayt of Dersingham, co. Norfolk, spinster, and Samuel Kerrich of the same place, D.D., and Barbara his wife. Rev. John Postlethwayt brother of the said Elizabeth and Barbara.

Manor of Denton Rectory. Special Court Baron of the Rev. William Chester, rector, held 14 May 1811, at the request of William Jenney, and Marianne Jenney, spinster, in the presence of John Steward, steward. Admission of William Jenney and Marianne Jenney, spinster, children of Edmund Jenney, deceased, by Elizabeth his late wife, deceased, on the surrender of Elizabeth Postle-thwayt, spinster, and Samuel Kerrich, D.D., and Barbara his wife. Reciting an extract from the will of John Van Kamp. " In order towards making a provision of mantainance for my two daughters, Tabitha and Susanna Maria, and the survivor of them, I devise unto the Rev. John Astley of Thornage, co. Norfolk, the Rev. Philip Bell, brother of Henry Bell, and William Jenney, son of Edmund Jenney, and the survivor of them all that my messuages, &c."

Manor of Denton Rectory. Special Court Baron of the Rev. William Chester, rector, held before the Lord himself on Tuesday, 14 May 1811, at the request of William Jenney and Marianne Jenney, spinster, in the presence of John Steward, steward. Admission of Gwyn Etheridge of Denton, co. Norfolk, on the surrender of William Jenney, and Marianne Jenney, in consideration of two hundred pounds.

Manor of Holbrooke, otherwise Alburgh. General Court Baron of John Wogan, held 27 January 1752, before Daniel Sayer, steward. Admission of John Van Kamp of Bungay, co. Suffolk, on the surrender of Elizabeth Postlethwayt of Dersingham, co. Norfolk, spinster, and Samuel Kerrich, D.D., and Barbara his wife.

Manor of Holbrooke, otherwise Alburgh. General Court Baron of John Wogan, Lord of the Manor, held 18 April 1756 before Daniel Sayer, steward. Admission of John Van Kamp of Bungay, co. Suffolk, on the surrender of William Bokenham, brother and heir of Lydia Bokenham.

Manor of Holbrooke, otherwise Alburgh. Special Court Baron of Mrs Rebecca Holmes, widow, Lady of the Manor, held 26 January 1801, before the Lady herself, in the presence of Thomas Smith, deputy steward. Admission of William Jenney, under the will of John Van Kamp, dated 2 March 1800.

Manor of Holbrooke, otherwise Alburgh. General Court Baron of Mrs Rebecca Holmes, widow, Lady of the Manor, held 24 November 1808, before George Clubbe Parsons, steward. Admission of the Rev. Philip Bell and William Jenney, under the will of John Van Kamp.

Manor of Topcroft with Denton. General Court Baron held 14 May 1742. Admission of Anthony Freston of St Cross, South Elmham, yeoman, on the surrender of the Rev. Thomas Stubbs.

Manor of Topcroft, with Denton. General Court Baron held 15 October 1751. Admission of John Van Kamp on the surrender of Samuel Kerrich, D.D., and Barbara his wife, and Elizabeth Postlethwayt.

Manor of Topcroft with Denton. General Court Baron held 21 April 1801. Admission of William Jenney under the will of John Van Kamp.

Manor of Topcroft with Denton. Special Court Baron held 15 May 1811. Admission of Gwyn Etheridge of Denton, on the surrender of William and Marianne Jenney.

Manor of Topcroft with Denton. Special Court Baron held 15 May 1811. Admission of William Jenney and Marianne Jenney, spinster, under the will of John Van Kamp.

Manor of Topcroft with Denton. General Court Baron held 20 June 1815. Admission of Gwyn Etheridge on the surrender of Anthony Freston.

Manor of Redenhall. General Court Baron of John Wogan, Lord of the Manor, held 27 January 1752 before Daniel Sayer, steward. Admission of John Van Kamp, on the surrender of Elizabeth Postlethwayt of Dersingham, spinster, Samuel Kerrich, D.D., and Barbara his wife.

Manor of Redenhall. Special Court Baron of Mrs Rebecca Holmes, widow, Lady of the Manor, held on Monday, 26 January 1801, in the presence of Thomas Smith, deputy steward. Admission of William Jenney, under the will of John Van Kamp.

From a volume in my possession, lettered, " Admissions to Manors in Redenhall and Denton, co. Norfolk."
—F. A. C.

Monumental Inscriptions in the Church at Birchington, co. Kent.

ELIZ: DAUG^R OF
MR JOHN AYLING
& ELIZ: HIS WIFE
WHO DIED OCT^R
THE 1ST 1678 AGED
6 YEARS.

On a small stone in the Quex Chapel.

BENEATH THIS STONE LIETH
THE REMAINS OF ELIZ: ROBERTS
WIFE OF W^M ROBERTS ESQ^R
WHO DIED 28TH OF SEPT^R 1788
AGED 45 YEARS.
ALSO THE SAID W^M ROBERTS ESQ^{RE}
WHO DIED 6TH OF JAN^Y 1805
AGED 82 YEARS.

On a flat stone in the Quex Chapel.

HERE LYETH INTERR'D $\frac{E}{Y}$ BODY OF
WILLIAM BVLLER ESQ^R OF
QUEAX IN THE COUNTY OF KENT
WHO DEPARTED THIS LIFE Y^E 30TH
OCT^R 1708 AGED 34 YEARS HE
MARRIED TO WIFE ELIZABETH ELDEST DAV-
GHTER OF RICHARD MEAD ESQ.
OF LONDON BY WHOM HE
HAD NO ISSUE.

On a flat stone in the Quex Chapel. Above are the Arms: On a cross, quarter-pierced, four eagles displayed, a crescent for difference, BULLER; impaling, A chevron between three pelicans vulning themselves, MEAD. Crest: A Moor's head couped, wreathed about the temples.

HEERE LYETH $\frac{E}{Y}$ BODY OF ANNE $\frac{E}{Y}$
WIFE OF ROGER SMITH GENT. &
THIRD DAVGHTER OF S^R ANTHONY
COLEPEPER OF BEDSBVRY K^T WHO
LEFT THIS LIFE FEB. 26, 1636.

On a flat stone in the Quex Chapel.

THIS MONUMENT IS ERECTED
TO THE MEMORY OF
CAPTAIN ARTHUR ANNESLEY COTTON
OF THE 7TH HUSSARS
BY THE OFFICERS OF THAT REGIMENT
AS A TESTIMONY OF THEIR SINCERE REGARD AND ESTEEM
FOR HIM AS A BROTHER OFFICER
AND COMPANION.
HE DIED THE 12TH OF MAY 1836.
AGED 24 YEARS.

*In the Quex Chapel, on a tablet on the south wall, between
the arches opening into the chancel.*

SACRED
TO THE MEMORY OF
CHARLOTTE
THE BELOVED WIFE OF
JOHN POWELL POWELL ESQ^{RE}
OF QUEX PARK, ISLE OF THANET
DIED 9TH AUGUST 1844.   AGED 70 YEARS
ALSO OF THE ABOVE NAMED
JOHN POWELL POWELL ESQ^{RE}
WHO DIED AT QUEX PARK
THE 14TH OF MAY 1849.   AGED 79 YEARS.

*In the Quex Chapel, on a tablet on the west wall.   Above are the
Arms: A lion rampant; impaling, On a chevron between three swans'
heads erased, as many trefoils slipped.   Crest: A dexter hand holding a
dagger.*

NEAR THIS STONE
LIETH THE REMAINS OF
WILLIAM ROBERTS ESQ^{RE}
OF KINGS GATE IN THE ISLE OF THANET
WHO DIED 6TH OF JAN^Y 1805
AGED 82 YEARS
ALSO ELIZTH ROBERTS HIS WIFE
WHO DIED 28 SEPT^R 1788
AGED 45 YEARS.
IN MEMORY LIKEWISE OF
ARTHUR ANNESLEY POWELL
ESQ^R THEIR ELDEST SON.   HE
DIED AT WHERWELL HANTS
JUNE THE 28TH 1813
ANNO ÆTAT. 47º.

In the Quex Chapel, on an oval tablet on the south wall.

IN A VAULT BENEATH THIS STONE
LIES INTERR'D THE BODY OF JOHN THE
SON OF JOHN AND MARTHA NEAME
OF GOAR END IN THIS PARISH
HE DIED MARCH THE 17TH 1765 AGED
EIGHT YEARS AND 11 MONTHS.
HAPPY THE BABE WHO PRIVILED'D BY FATE
TO SHORTEN LABOUR AND A LIGHTER WEIGHT
RECEIV'D BUT YESTERDAY THE GIFT OF BREATH
ORDERED TO-MORROW TO RETURN TO DEATH.
ALSO IN THE SAME VAULT IS INTERR'D THE
BODY OF MR WILLIAM MOCKETT LATE OF
DANDELION IN THIS ISLE, WHO DIED THE 27TH
OF JULY 1771 AGED 73 YEARS.

On a flat stone in the south chancel.

SACRED
TO THE MEMORY OF
HARRIOT WIFE OF CHARLES BOWLAND COTTON ESQ^{RE}
OF KINGSGATE IN THE ISLE OF THANET
WHO DIED ON THE 18TH DAY OF JANUARY 1837 AGED 60 YEARS
AND OF SEVEN OF THEIR CHILDREN
ARTHUR HENRY BULLER WHO DIED 4 AUGST 1804 AGED 11 DAYS
ARTHUR HENRY BULLER WHO DIED 8 OCT. 1806 AGED ONE YEAR
LAURA SUSAN WHO DIED 31 MARCH 1811 AGED 12 YEARS
ALEXANDRINA WHO DIED 16 SEP^R 1815 AGED 12 DAYS
HARRIOT POWELL WHO DIED 6 JUNE 1819 AGED 11 YEARS
CHARLES WILLIAM, A LIEUTENANT IN THE 5TH NATIVE CAVALRY
WHO DIED AT SHALAPORE IN THE EAST INDIES
ON THE 15TH NOVEMBER 1821 AGED 19 YEARS
AT WHICH PLACE A MONUMENT HAS BEEN ERECTED TO HIS MEMORY
BY AND AT THE EXPENSE OF HIS BROTHER OFFICERS
ARTHUR ANNESLEY VALENTIA A CAPTAIN IN THE 7TH HUSSARS
WHO DIED 12 MAY 1836 AGED 24 YEARS
AND TO WHOSE MEMORY A MONUMENT HAS BEEN ERECTED IN THIS CHURCH
BY HIS BROTHER OFFICERS AT THEIR OWN REQUEST AND EXPENSE
ALSO OF THE ABOVE NAMED
CHARLES BOWLAND COTTON ESQ^R OF KINGSGATE
WHO DIED SEPTEMBER 5TH 1847
IN THE 80TH YEAR OF HIS AGE.

In the Quex Chapel, on the north wall.   Below is a Crest:
A griffin's head erased, pierced with an arrow.

HEER LYETH INTERRED
THE BODY OF IONE THE
DAVGHTER OF RICHARD
SIMONS OF TYLMANSTONE
LATE THE WIFE OF
THOMAS KIRBY OF SOVTHEND
WHO DEPARTED THIS
LIFE THE 82 YEARE OF
HVR AGE IVNE THE 13
ANO DOMI 1656.

On a flat stone in the nave

HERE LYETH THE BODY OF IOHN
AVSTEN YEOMAN OF MINSTER HE
DEPARTED THIS LIFE THE 21 OF
IANUARY   .   .   .

On a ledger stone in the aisle, near the west door.

---

*On a ledger stone an inscription of several lines, the only word
of which is legible is* KERBY.

HERE ALSO LIETH INTERR'D THE
BODY OF IOHN KERBY OF VILL OF
WOOD OF THIS PARISH KENSMAN
TO THE ABOVE SAID JOHN KERBY
WHO DEPARTED THIS LIFE THE 14TH
DAY OF IUNE IN THE YEAR OF OUR
LORD 1717 ÆTATIS 66 YEARS.

On a flat stone in the nave.

HERE LIETH INTERRED THE BODY
OF THOMAS KIRBY OF SOUTHEND
WHO DEPED THIS LIFE THE FIRST
DAY OF MARCH ANNO Dñi 1651,
AND IN THE 78TH YEARE OF HIS
AGE, HE MARIED IOANE $\frac{E}{Y}$ DAVGHTER
OF RICHARD SIMONS OF TILMESTON
AND BY HER HAD ISSVE 5 SONNS
AND ONE DAVGHTER OF WHOME
THE 2 YONGEST SONNS PAVLL AND
THOMAS ARE YETT SVRVIVING.

On a flat stone in the nave.

40

Hic iacet Iohes Turk qui obijt xxj die Octobr Anno
M. ... ...
... ...

HERE LIETH INTERR'D
Y^E BODIES OF MR GEORGE FRIEND
OF THIS PARISH AND MARGARY
HIS WIFE HE DEPARTED THIS LIFE
Y^E 18TH DAY OF SEPTEMBER 1703
AGED 71 YEARS, AND SHE DEPARTED
THIS LIFE Y^E 18TH DAY OF IANUARY 1704
ÆTATIS 82 YEARS.

On a flat stone in the nave.

———————

HERE LYES INTERR'D Y^E BODYS OF M^R
THO^S VNDERDOWN, LATE OF FORDWICH
(THRICE MAYOR OF THAT CORPORATION)
& ANN HIS WIFE WHO HAD ISSUE
BY HER 1 SON & 4 DAUGHTERS HE
DIED JAN^Y Y^E 8TH 1709 AGED 66 YEARS
SHE DIED SEP^R Y^E 14TH 1690
AGED 49 YEARS.

On a flat stone in the nave.

———————

IN HOPES OF A JOYFUL
RESURRECTION
HERE LIETH THE BODY
OF JOHN GOARE
WHO DEPARTED THIS
LIFE MARCH THE 19TH
1754 AGED 62 YEARS.

On a ledger stone in the south aisle.

———————

HERE UNDER LIETH THE BODY
OF HENERY AUSTEN IN HOPE
OF A BLESSED RESURRECTION
. . OF OCTOBER IN THE YEERE
OF OUR LORD ONE THOUSAND
SIX HVNDRED SIXTY AND
ONE.

———————

𝕳𝖎𝖈 𝖎𝖆𝖈𝖊𝖙 𝕵𝖔𝖍𝖊𝖘 𝕼𝖚𝖊𝖐 𝖖𝖚𝖎 𝖔𝖇𝖎𝖏𝖙 𝖝𝖝𝖎° 𝖉𝖎𝖊 𝕺𝖈𝖙𝖔𝖇𝖗 𝕵° 𝕯𝖚𝖎
𝖒𝖈𝖈𝖈𝖈°𝖝𝖑𝖎𝖝.

*On a brass on the floor of the Quex Chapel. Above
are two effigies.*

NEAR ARE DEPOSITED THE REMAINS OF
SARAH WIFE OF JAMES NEAME,
WHO DEPARTED THIS LIFE THE 4TH OF APRIL
1803 AGED 49 YEARS.
ALSO ANN DAUGHTER OF THE ABOVE WHO DEPARTED
THIS LIFE THE 26TH OF JULY 1795 AGED 14 YEARS.
THOSE LIKEWISE OF MR JAMES NEAME
SECOND SON OF THE ABOVE HE DIED
APRIL THE 8TH 1814, ANNO ÆTAT. 29°
ALSO SARAH THIRD DAUGHTER OF THE ABOVE
WHO DIED JUNE 24TH 1822 AGED 42 YEARS.
ALSO THE ABOVE JAMES NEAME
WHO DIED JUNE 30TH 1843 AGED 97 YEARS.
ALSO CHARLOTTE NEAME
DAUGHTER OF THE ABOVE
WHO DIED SEPR 2ND 1872 AGED 79 YEARS.
ALSO MARIA NEAME,
DAUGHTER OF THE ABOVE JAMES NEAME
WHO DIED DECR 3RD 1879 AGED 91 YEARS.

On a monument on the south wall.

IN A VAULT NEAR THIS PLACE LIE THE BODIES OF
JOHN FRIEND AND MARY HIS WIFE
HE DIED AUGUST THE 4TH 1792 AGED 71 YEARS
AND SHE DIED OCTOBER 26TH 1784 AGED 61 YEARS.
ALSO MARY WIFE OF JOHN FRIEND JUNR WHO DIED
THE 20TH OF SEPTEMBER 1793 AGED 40 YEARS.
ALSO MARY DAUGHTER OF THE ABOVE JOHN AND MARY FRIEND
WHO DIED MARCH THE 18TH 1801 AGED 17 YEARS.
ALSO SARAH DAUGHTER OF GEORGE AND PHEEBE FRIEND
WHO DIED MARCH THE 3RD 1807 AGED 22 YEARS.
ALSO THE REV. HENRY FRIEND, LATE VICAR OF
EAST FARLEIGH IN THIS COUNTY DIED AUGT 5TH 1811 AGED 53 YEARS.
ALSO PHOEBE WIFE OF GEORGE FRIEND ABOVE NAMED,
DIED MAY 14TH 1812, AGED 52 YEARS.
ALSO GEORGE FRIEND ESQR OF THIS PARISH DIED
NOVR 5TH 1813 AGED 66 YEARS.
ALSO JOHN FRIEND ESQR LATE OF BROOKS END
IN THIS PARISH DIED APRIL THE 3RD 1817
AGED 64 YEARS.

On a marble monument on the west wall, north aisle.

42

THE
RIGHTEOUS
HATH HOPE
IN HIS
DEATH.
PROV^S XIV. 32.
A RECORD.
SACRED TO JAMES TOMLIN
OF WEST MALLING IN THIS COUNTY
ESQUIRE AND TO THE
AFFECTION OF HIS WIDOW JANE
HE DIED JAN^Y 21ST 1846
AGED 68 YEARS.
DURING THE EARLIER PART
OF LIFE HE WAS A MERCHANT OF
LONDON, AND FOR MORE THAN
THIRTY YEARS A MEMBER OF
THE COURT OF THE GOLDSMITHS
COMPANY IN THAT CITY.
SACRED ALSO TO THE MEMORY
OF HIS FATHER WILLIAM TOMLIN
WHO DIED APRIL 11TH 1789 AGED 44.
OF HIS MOTHER SUSANNAH TOMLIN
WHO DIED APRIL 9TH 1830 AGED 81.
OF HIS ELDEST BROTHER JOHN TOMLIN
WHO DIED MARCH 21ST 1838 AGED 66.
ALL OF WHOM RESIDED IN THIS PARISH
OF HIS NEPHEW WILLIAM TOMLIN
OF LONDON ; MERCHANT ; SON OF
THE ABOVE JOHN TOMLIN,
WHO DIED AT LIEGE IN BELGIUM,
MAY 25TH 1841 AGED 31 YEARS,
AND WAS BURIED IN
A VAULT NEAR THIS CHURCH BY
THE SIDE OF HIS FATHER.
ALSO OF JANE, WIDOW OF THE ABOVE
JAMES TOMLIN
WHO DIED AT NORTHDOWN
JANUARY 28TH 1880, AGED 85 YEARS.

On a monument on the west wall, south aisle. Below are the Arms: On a chevron between three battle-axes as many right hands in armour, TOMLIN ; *impaling, Quarterly: 1st and 4th,* TOMLIN ; *2nd, On a bend a man's head in armour ; 3rd, A chevron between three mullets pierced. Crest: A right hand in armour between two battle-axes in saltire. Motto : Æquabiliter et diligenter.*

––––––––––

SAMUEL BROOKE ESQ^R
DIED JUNE 11TH 1774.

On a ledger stone in the nave.

43

IN A VAULT NEAR THIS MONUMENT
ERECTED BY JOHN GRETTON OF PECKHAM
IN THE COUNTY OF SURREY ESQ^R
IS DEPOSITED THE BODY OF SARAH HIS FIRST WIFE
WHO WAS THE WIDOW
OF EBENEZER NUSSELL ESQ^R
SHE DIED OF A CANCER JAN^{RY} 28TH 1775 AGED 35
ALSO THE BODY OF MARY HER UNMARRIED SISTER WHO DIED OF THE SAME
DREADFULL MALADY MAY 12TH 1777 AGED 35
AND OF NICHOLAS STRIVENS (OF THIS PARISH) THEIR FATHER
WHO DIED APRIL 16TH 1780 AGED 58.

On a monument on the south wall.

HERE LIES INTERR'D THE BODY OF
SARAH WIFE OF GEORGE FRIEND
OF THIS PARISH LEFT ISSUE THREE
SONS AND TWO DAUGHTERS VIZ:
JOHN, GEO^E & HENRY, ELIZABETH
AND ANN.   SHE DEPARTED THIS LIFE
THE 7TH OF JULY 1741 AGED 49 YEARS.
ALSO THE BODY OF THE ABOVE
GEORGE FRIEND WHO DIED THE
2^D OF JUNE 1761 AGED 72 YEARS.

On a ledger stone in the nave.

𝔥𝔦𝔠 𝔯𝔢𝔮𝔲𝔦𝔢𝔰𝔠𝔦𝔱 𝔐𝔞𝔤𝔢𝔰𝔱𝔦𝔯 𝔍𝔬𝔥𝔢𝔰 𝔥𝔢𝔶𝔫𝔶𝔰 𝔠𝔩𝔢𝔯𝔦𝔠𝔲𝔰
𝔫𝔲𝔭𝔢𝔯 𝔙𝔦𝔠𝔞𝔯𝔦𝔲𝔰 𝔡𝔢 𝔐𝔬𝔫𝔨𝔱𝔬𝔫 𝔮𝔲𝔦 𝔬𝔟𝔦𝔧𝔱 𝔫𝔬𝔫𝔬 𝔡𝔦𝔢 𝔒𝔠𝔱𝔬-
𝔟𝔯𝔢𝔰 𝔞𝔫𝔫𝔬 𝔡𝔫𝔦 𝔪^d𝔳^c𝔵𝔵𝔦𝔦𝔧.

On a brass in the nave.   Above is the figure of a priest.

HERE ARE DEPOSITED
THE REMAINS OF
FRANCIS NEAME AND
ELIZABETH HIS WIFE
HE DIED 11TH OCT^R 1759
AGED 47 YEARS.
SHE DIED 7TH SEP. 1807
AGED 97 YEARS.
ALSO ANN THEIR DAUGHTER
DIED 29 NOV. . . .
AGED 2 YEARS.
ALSO FRANCIS SMITH
AN INFANT
THEIR GRANDSON
THEY HAD ISSUE VIZ:
JOHN, WILLIAM, JAMES,
ELIZABETH, MARY & ANN.

On a ledger stone near the south door.

Hic requiescit Magister Johannes Herrys Alexiensis ... ... de Moulton qui obiit nono die ... ... anno dni M⁰V⁰ ... ...

IN MEMORY OF RICHARD
WILLSON WHO DIED NOV^R
THE 14TH 1769. ALSO OF MARY
HIS WIFE WHO DIED AUGUST
THE 27TH 1765.
ALSO SARAH THEIR
DAUGHTER WHO DIED NOV^R
THE 12TH 1794 AGED 66 YEARS.

On a ledger stone in the south aisle.

———————

JAMES THORNTON
DIED 6 OCT : 1811
AGED 3 YEARS
AND 6 MONTHS.

On a ledger stone near the font.

———————

DOROTHY MARSDEN
DIED 24TH DEC^R 1811 AGED 16 YEARS.
ELIZABETH MARSDEN
DIED 28TH FEB^Y 1816 AGED 21 YEARS.

On a ledger stone in the nave.

———————

IN MEMORY
OF M^{RS} ELIZABETH TOMLIN
OF MARGATE RELICT
OF MR CORNELIUS TOMLIN
WHO DEPARTED THIS LIFE
THE 31ST OF JAN^Y 1802
AGED 75 YEARS.

On a ledger stone in the south aisle.

———————

SACRED
TO THE MEMORY OF
JOHN SIDDERS OF THIS
PARISH WHO DIED JAN^Y 30, 1810
AGED 55 YEARS.
ALSO MARY WIFE OF THE
ABOVE JOHN SIDDERS WHO
DIED APRIL 16TH 1817 AGED 62 YEARS.
ALSO MARTHA, DAUGHTER
OF THE ABOVE JOHN AND MARY
SIDDERS WHO DIED FEB^Y 19TH 1828
AGED 36 YEARS.

On a ledger stone in the north aisle.

IN A VAULT BENEATH ARE DEPOSITED
THE REMAINS OF JAMES FRIEND ESQ^{RE}
OB : AUGUST 3RD 1819 ANNO ÆTAT. 39°
ALSO THE BODY OF EDW^D FRIEND ESQ^{RE}
OF LONDON
OB : APRIL 22ND 1820 ÆTAT. 27°
ALSO THE BODY OF
HENRIETTA WHITELEY,
OB : OCTOBER 29TH ÆTAT. 23°
ALSO THE BODY OF ELIZTH BOULTON,
OB : FEBRUARY 17TH 1821 ÆTAT. 33°
DAUGHTERS OF THE LATE GEO^E FRIEND ESQ^{RE}
OF THIS PARISH.

On a mural tablet on the north wall of the north aisle.

IN THE FAMILY VAULT BENEATH
LIE THE REMAINS OF ELIZABETH FRIEND OF THIS PARISH
OB : FEBRUARY 23RD 1827 ÆT. 76.
ALSO OF MARY, WIFE OF EDWARD TADDY ESQ^R OF MARGATE
AND SISTER OF THE ABOVE NAMED OB : OCTOBER 31ST 1828 ÆT. 70.
ALSO OF GEORGE FRIEND ESQUIRE OF LONDON
FORMERLY OF THIS PARISH, OB : JULY 31ST 1831 ÆT. 41
ALSO OF SARAH, RELICT OF UPTON JENNINGS ESQUIRE.
FORMERLY OF FORDWICH,
AND SISTER OF THE FIRST NAMED, OB : MARCH 4TH 1834 ÆT. 84
ALSO OF MARY ANN FRIEND LATE OF THIS PARISH
OB : APRIL 6TH 1834, ÆT. 51.
ALSO OF GEORGE TWYMAN FRIEND ESQUIRE
OB : NOVEMBER 27TH 1836, ÆT. 45
ALSO OF SARAH WIFE OF EDWARD HATFEILD ESQUIRE
OB : AUGUST 15TH 1846 ÆT. 61.
ALSO OF MARGARET, WIFE OF JOHN FRIEND ESQUIRE,
OB : FEBRUARY 21ST 1856 ÆT. 81.
ALSO OF JOHN FRIEND ESQUIRE OF BROOKS END
OB : JULY 4TH 1858, ÆT. 70.

On a mural monument in the north aisle.

TO THE MEMORY OF THOMAS GREY OF BIRCHINGTON HALL IN THIS PARISH.
WHO DIED 28TH FEB^{RY} 1879 AGED 50 AND LIES BURIED IN KENSAL GREEN CEMETARY.

THESE WINDOWS WERE PUT IN BY HIS SORROWING WIDOW SUSAN GRAY.

Memorial windows on north side of nave.

IN MEMORY OF HARRIET 3RD
DAUGHTER OF THE LATE ROBERT
TOMLIN OF NORTHDOWN ESQ^{RE}
DIED 4TH MAY 1875, AGED 78.

Memorial window on north side of nave.

———

IN MEMORY OF JOHN FRIEND ESQ. OBIT JULY 19TH 1858 AGED 77.

Memorial window on north side of nave. Above are the Arms: Gules,
a fess nebuly ermine between six billets or. Crest: On a mount vert
an eagle with wings displayed argent. Motto: Alis volat propriis.

———

A crest: A lion passant. Motto: Celer atque fidelis.

A crest: A snake's head between two ostrich feathers. Motto: Vive
ut vivas.

———

TO THE GLORY OF GOD AND IN
AFFECTIONATE MEMORY OF
LOUISA BURROUGHES WIFE
OF JAMES COLLIS BIRD WHO
DIED SEP. 17, 1891. THIS
WINDOW IS ERECTED BY HER
LOVING HUSBAND AND CHILDREN.

Memorial window on south side of nave.

———

TO THE GLORY OF GOD & IN
MEMORY OF MY DEAR SON
GABRIEL CHA^S DANTE
ROSSETTI. BORN IN
LONDON MAY 12, 1828 DIED
AT BIRCHINGTON EASTER DAY
1882.

Memorial window on south side of nave.

47

I. M. O.
WILLIAM SCOTT OF LYNN, NORFOLK
DIED 15 DEC^R 1857 AGED 62 YEARS.

I. M. O.
ELIZABETH SPRY HIS DAUGHTER
WHO DIED 10 JUNE 1873.

I. M. O.
WILLIAM SCOTT JUN^R OF LYNN, NORFOLK
DIED FEB^Y 2ND 1869 AGED 42 YEARS.

I. M. O.
ALFRED JOICE SCOTT HIS SON & NEPHEW OF THO^S GRAY
DIED IN RANGOON, B. BURMAH, 28TH OCT. 1872, AGED 21 YEARS.

---

*On a small brass between the first and second windows from the east
on the south side.*

THESE FOUR WINDOWS
WERE GIVEN BY THOMAS
GRAY OF BIRCHINGTON
HALL.

IN MEMORY OF THOMAS
GREY DIED 15TH JUNE
1864 AGED 75 AND
MARY HIS WIFE DIED 10TH
JUNE 1857 AGED 53
ALSO MARY THEIR
DAUGHTER DIED 22ND
AUGUST 1849 AGED 24.

On the west window.

*The inscriptions in Birchington Church relating to members of the
Crispe family are printed in the " Family of Crispe," Vol. 4,
and the above are all the other inscriptions I could find in the
Church when I made notes there in September 1896.--F. A. C.*

48

Partridge Family.

𝕿𝖔 𝖆𝖑𝖑 𝕮𝖍𝖗𝖎𝖘𝖙𝖎𝖆𝖓 𝕻𝖊𝖔𝖕𝖑𝖊 To Whome this presente Wrightinge shall
Come Robarte Partridge of Stoake by Nayland in the Countye of Suff
yeoman Sendeth Greetinge In o^r Lord God euerlastinge Knowe yee that
I the saide Robarte Partridge, Aswell ffor the loue and affection Which
I haue and beare, To Elisabeth my nowe wiffe as allso ffor and towards
the future mayntainance of my saide wiffe after my decease, And likewise
for divers other good Causes and Consideracions my selfe therevnto
moueinge Haue given graunted enffeoffed and Confirmed, And by
these p^rsents Doe give, graunte, enffeoffe and Confirme To John Crispe
of little Cornerd in the Countye of Suffolcke yeoman, John Wilkin
of the same Towne and Countye yeoman, And John Crispe Junio^r of
Bures St Marye in the Countye of Suff aforesaide Cardwiner All that
my Messuage or Tẽmente Wherein I doe nowe dwell, Called Roodings,
With A Garden Orchard, And all and euery the Barnes, stable howses
and buildings Whatsoeuer to the saide Messuage or Tẽmente beinge
and belonginge, And likewise Eight Acres of Arable lande (more or less)
beinge in one parcell Called Roodings allso, Or by Whatsoeuer other
name or names the same are Called and knowne, To the same
Tenemente beinge, and belonginge As the same and euery of them are
sett lyeinge and beinge in Stoake by Nayland aforesaide, In the Tenure
and occupacion of mee the said Robarte Partridge Abuttinge vpon the
Church Yarde of the same parrish Church and Certaine Tenements in
parte towards the South, The high waye leadinge ffrom Stoake aforesaide
towards Sudbury on the North in parte, Vpon the highwaye leadinge
ffrom Stoake aforesaide towards Polstedd on the East, And vpon a
street Called Puttocke streett, Towards the West, together with all and
euery the Rights pfitts, Rents, and Comodities of Righte beinge and
belonginge Or in any Wise appteyneinge to the said Messuage or
Tenemente, All and euery which saide Messuage or Tenemente and
parcell of lande With their apptenances I late had to my selfe and my
heires (amongst other things) By the last Will and Testamente of
Thomas Partridge my late ffather deceased As in and by the same Will
and Testamente doeth and maye appeare, And which saide messuage
or Tenemente, and Eight Acres of lande With All and euery their
apptenances my saide ffather had and purchased amongst other things of
One Richard Monyngs of Stoake aforesaide yeoman, As in and by the
deed poll in Wrightinge of the saide Richard Monyngs graunted
(beareinge date the two & twentieth daye of August In the two and
ffortyeth yeare of the Raigne of o^r late Soue^raigne Ladye Queene
Elisabeth maye playnlye appeare, To haue and to holde All and singular
the saide messuage or Tẽmente, Garden Orchard and all and euery the
Barnes stable howses and buildings Whatsoeuer With the Eight Acres of
Lande And together with the Comodyties, Rights, pfitts and appptenances
in any Wise to the same, appteyneinge and belonginge To the sayde
John Crispe senio^r John Wilkin and John Crispe Junio^r their heires and
Assignes To the vse and behoof of my selfe and Elisabeth my saide
Wiffe ffor terme of o^r Naturall lives, and of the Naturall liffe of the
longer liver of vs both And ffrom and after the decease of the Surviveor
of vs both To the heires of the bodye of the saide Elisabeth my saide
wiffe By me begotten or to be begotten And for the Wante of such

49

yssue of our bodyes To the Righte and nexte heire of mee the saide
Robarte Partridge, fforeuer, Of the Chieffe Lorde or Lordes of the ffee
thereof By the Rents and services therfore of right due and accustomed
And I the saide Robarte Partridge for my selfe and my heires All and
singular the saide Messuage, Garden, Orchard, Eight Accres of Lande,
howses, buildings pfitts, Rights Comodities and p'misses With the
apptenances Whatsoeuer, To the saide John Crispe, John Wilkin, and
John Crispe, Junior their heires and Assignes, To the vse and vses aboue
limytted and exp'ssed, Against my selfe and my heires, And all and any
other pson, and psons Claymeinge, by ffrom or under mee, Doe, shall
and will warrante and foreuer defende by these p'sents And moreouer I
the saide Robarte Partridge for my selfe, and my heires, Doe hereby
Couenante pmise and graunte, To and With the saide John Crispe
thelder, John Wilkin, and John Crispe the younger, Thatt the sayde
Messuage, Garden Orchard, Eight Acres of lande With the houses,
buildings, and apptenances aforemencioned and euery of them, And the
Seisen, state and possession thereof by mee had taken, and deliuered
the daye of the date hereof, To the saide John Crispe, John Wilkin, and
John Crispe, (to the vses abouesaide) shall from tyme to tyme, and att all
tymes hearafter, be sufficientlye and Cleerlye exonerated acquitted and
discharged, ffrom all and euerey former bargaine, sale, Acte or Actes, deed,
Lease, and Leases Mortgages & encombrances Whatsoeuer, Claymed, or
to be Claymed, by ffrom or under mee, or my Acte Consente or
pcurement (The Rents and services abouemencioned exceepted) And
that The graunted p'misses With all and euery the Apptenances shalbe
and Remaine To the vse and vses aboue expressed, accordinge to the
true meaneinge intente & purpose of this presente deed of ffeoffmente.
In Wittness Whereof and for the true and suer pformance I the saide
Robarte Partridge haue herevnto putt my hande and seale The
ffouerteenth daye of Januarye In the Tenth Yeare of the Raigne of o'
Soue'aigne Lord Kinge Charles By the Grace of God of Englande
Scotland ffraunce and Ireland, Defender of the ffayth &c. Annoque
Dni: 1634.

The Obligacion is 200li.

The Condicion of this Obligacion w'hin Written is Wharas the Within
bounden, Robarte Partridge, by his deed of ffeoffmente Hath enffeoffed
and Assuered To the With named John Crispe thelder John Wilkin of
little Cornerd in the Countye of Suff yeoman and John Crispe Junio'
All this his Messuage With thapptenances and eight Acres of Lande
sett lyeinge and beinge in Stoake w'hin written, Called by the name and
names of Roodings and nowe in the occupacion of the same Robarte
Partridge, To the vse of the same Robarte Partridge and Elisabeth his
nowe wiffe ffor terme of their naturall lives and of the liffe of the longer
liver of them, And after the decease of the Surviver of them both To the
heires of the bodye of the same Elisabeth begotten, or to be begotten, by
the same Robart Partridge as in and by his deed poll beareinge date the
daye of the date hereof maye and doeth appeare, Yf therefore the same
Elisabeth nowe Wiffe of the saide Robarte Partridge shall and maye

haue holde possesse & inioye the saide Messuage With all and euery the mencioned apptenances, and the eight Acres of Lande thervnto belonginge, ffrom and after the decease of the aforesaide Robarte Partridge, ffor and dueringe the naturall liffe of the same Elisabeth. And allso thatt the heires of the bodye of the same Elisabeth begotten Or to be begotten, by the same Robarte Partridge, shall and maye haue holde and enioye, The saide Messuage and eight Acres of Lande With thapptenances, ffrom and affter the decease of the same Robarte and Elisabeth Partridge, and of the longer liver of them both, According to the true meaneinge intente and purpose of the mencioned Deed of ffeoffmente, That then this presente Obligacion Within Written To be vtterlye voyde and of none efecte Or els to remaine in full force & vertu.

Wittnessed by Mathewe Howe
Henrye Hedge and Susan Hull.

Sealed and deliuered and Sessen State and peaceable possession of the Within mencioned p^{r}misses was had and taken by the within named Robarte Partridge The daye and yeare Within Written And deliuered the same daye by the same Robarte Partridge To the wthin written John Crispe senio^r according to the true meaneinge intente & purpose of this p^{r}sente deed of ffeoffmente To the vse therein mencioned. In the p^{r}sence of.

Memorand that the true meaneinge of this p^{r}sente Deed of ffeoffement is That The parte of the mencioned Eight Acrees of lande & ye Tement neere adioyneinge to the graunted p^{r}misses & nowe in the occupacion of the saide Robarte Partridge named in the same deed beinge latlye Recouered and had by the heire of Thomas Partridge Junio^r deceased is nott to be deemed had, taken or Claymed, as any parte parcell of the p^{r}misses graunted by the Contents of this p^{r}sente deed of ffeoffmente.

From a document in the possession of Charles S. Partridge of Stowmarket, Suffolk.—F. A. C.

Stonehouse, co. Gloucester.

. . DECEMBER 1653.

READER ABOVE THOV HAST THE YEARE
WHEREIN WE LOST A FRIEND MOST DEARE
WHEREIN IT PLEASDE GOD HENCE TO CALL
HIS FAITHFVLL SERVANT SAMVELL BALL
WHOSE NOBLE PARTE AND EXLENT WORTH
I CANNOT HERE AT ALL SETT FOORTH

HIS SOVLE ASPIRDE TO GOD ON HIGHE
HIS CORPES VNDER THIS TOMBE DOTH LYE
OVR LOSS OF HIM LET VS LAMENT
AND FOR OVR SINNS WITH SPEEDE REPENT
THAT SOE PREPARED WEE MAY DYE
TO LIVE WITH GOD ETERNALLY.

On the south side of an altar tomb in the churchyard, near north porch of church. The Register records his burial as follows: "1653. Samuel Ball the Elder was buried the seventh of December.—F. A. C.

Jones Family.

Ame Jones y^e ffirst borne Daughter of Samuell Jones and Ame his wife was borne at Woolwich y^e 3^d of ffebruary at 6 at night Anno: 167$\frac{6}{7}$ And departed this world on y^e 17th of septemb: ffollowing 1677 in Anchor in hope Alley & buried in St Katherines Church.

Ame Jones our second Daughter was borne on weddensday y^e 4th of September at $\frac{1}{2}$ an hour past 7 at night Anno: 1678 in Anchor and hope Alley. And baptized on Thursday y^e 19th day ffollowing by y^e Parson of St Katherines.

Samuell Jones our sone was born on Sabothday y^e 25th of July 1680 at 6 aclock in y^e morning.

Dina Jones our daughter was borne on thursday y^e 29th of July 1682 between 5 and 6 a clock at night and Christned ye same night Anno: 1682.

Ame Jones our 2^d Daughter Departed this world on ye 7th of September 1682 And buried on sunday ye 10th ffollowing in St Katherines Church Chancell.

Samuell Jones our sone Departed this world on ye 22^d of September 1682 and buried on munday y^e 25th ffollowing in y^e same grave with our Daughter Ame.

Sarah Jones our Daughter was born on tuesday at 3 aclock in y^e morneing being y^e 7th day of August 1683.

Samuell Jones our second sone was borne on ffryday y^e 18th day of December 1685 at some what above $\frac{1}{2}$ an hour past four in y^e Affternoone and baptized betwix^t 8 and 9 aclock y^e same night.

Joseph Jones and Benjamin Jones sones of Samuell and Ame Jones his wife were borne y^e 19th of Aprill being thursday at 5 in y^e morneing 1688.

Joseph Jones son of Samuell and Ame Jones his wife departed this Life ye 30th of Aprill 1688. Buried ye 3^d of May ffollowing in Stepney Churchyard.

Benjamin Jones sone of Samuell and Ame Jones was baptized y^e 3^d of May and dyed about y^e 11th of y^e said mounth and buried by his brother in y^e south side of Stepney churchyard.

George Jones sone of Samuell and Ame Jones his wife was born on saterday y^e 14th of September 1689 at $\frac{1}{2}$ an hour Past one of y^e clock at noon and baptized by Mr Garrat of St. Katherines y^e 8th of October ffollowing.

Ame Jones Daughter of Samuell and Ame Jones his wife was borne y^e 16th of September being thursday betwixt 8 & 9 in y^e evening 1690. And Baptized about 10 y^e same night by Mr Garrat Minister of St Katherines.

My Daughter Susanna Jones was borne November ye 16th 1693 at 7 a clock at night being thursday 1693.

From a volume containing a book of Common Prayer, Bible, &c., dated 1680, in my possession.—F. A. C.

Abstracts of Documents relating to the Town Estate and Charities of the Parish of Pakenham, Suffolk.

4th Edward IV. (146⁴⁄₅).

Thomas Spynneys and John Chylston of Thurston, demise to Maria Beman of Wolpet, and John Clement of Stowelangtote, three roods of meadow called Cobbeshyll, which they formerly held conjointly with William Abell of Pakenham of the feoffment of John Stobs and William Hye of Pakenham, to have and to hold for the aforesaid Mary and John Clement, their heirs and assigns. Witnesses:—William Smyth, William Hert, John Fouler, John Banyard, and John Fysshe, of Pakenham.

16th Edward IV. (147⁶⁄₇).

William Smyth of Pakenham demises to Robert Clerk, John Pryour, William Hert, and Thomas Cage, all of Pakenham, three pieces of arable land:—(1) Five acres and a half at Stalmer; (2) Three roods in Fowleslowe field, between the lands of the Cellarer of St Edmunds and the king's highway leading to Bury, and the land of the Manor of Netherhall; (3) Three roods in the same abutting on the land of Henry Straunge, esquire, formerly of Abell Beman, which pieces of land he lately held conjointly with William Smyth, Citizen and Scrivener of London, John Rous of Pakenham, John Walsham, lately of the same, and formerly of Norton by Wolpet, and John Seymour, deceased, of the demise and feoffment of Simon Ive, lately of Pakenham, John Cok, lately of Chevyngton, Robert Canham lately of Pakenham, and Thomas Maltiward, lately of Felsham, to have and to hold to them and their heirs, etc. Witnesses:—John Cage, Thomas Rose, Robert Gambown, Richard Crooke, John Byrd, Thomas Mayster, with many others.

17th Edward IV. (1477).

Exchange between Richard, Abbot of St Edmunds, the Prior and the Convent, on the one part, and Robert Clerke, Richard Abell, and John Pecok of Pakenham, on the other part. The latter give three acres arable in town and fields of Pakenham, of which one acre and a half lies in Apyscroftfeld, abutting east, west and south, on lands of Pakenham Hall, and north on Hellewey; half an acre lies in Netherapes-croftfeld, abutting north, east and west on said manor, and south upon Monkespath; another half acre lies in the same field, abutting north, east and west, on said manor, and south on Sheep Close; another half acre lies in Kanelowesfeld, abutting north and south-west on said manor, and east on Castellwey. In exchange for a certain pightle called Teyntowreyerd, parcel of the manor called Rycardes Hall in Pakenham aforesaid, in which pightle is being erected, builded, and completed by will and licence of the said Abbot, Prior and Convent, a certain house called "a chirchehous sive a Gyldehalle" for the use of the said townsfolk inhabitants of Pakenham for ever. On condition that the aforesaid three acres shall belong to the Manor of Pakenham Hall to the use and profit of the Cellarer of the said Monastery in exchange for two pieces of land containing by estimation four acres of arable, more or less, parcels of the Manor of Pakenham Hall, whereof one piece is reckoned for three acres and-a-half lying at Londongate, next the land of Thomas Rose on the west, and the king's highway called Lavenham wey on the east, one head abuts on the lands of William Aubry towards the south, and the other head on the king's highway called Bury wey, and on another piece of land, parcel of the same four acres towards the north. And the half acre lies in the same field next the king's highway, called Bury wey on the north, and the lands of divers men on the south. The east head abuts on the aforesaid three acres and-a-half, and the west head abuts on the aforesaid Manor of Pakenham Hall. And the said half acre is called Goryland, which two pieces, containing four acres, shall belong to the Manor called Rycardes Hall, to the use and profit of the Treasurer of the said Monastery, or of the Supervisor of the said Manor in exchange for the aforesaid three acres, for which four acres the Treasurer of the said Monastery or the Supervisor of the said Manor called Rycardes Hall shall pay yearly to the Manor of Pakenham Hall threepence at the two terms of the year, Easter and Michaelmas, in equal portions. The two parts of this Indenture sealed by the parties respectively in the Chapter House of Bury on the 1st of June in the 17th year of King Edward the Fourth after the Conquest.

2nd HENRY VII. (1486).

Robert Clerke, Richard Abell, and John Pecok of Pakenham, give to Henry Cage of Pakenham, Robert Cage, John Hert, William Crysten of Grymston, Thomas Holdder, William Pryour, Walter Pecok, John Clerke, junior, John Herne, Benedict Fordham, Thomas Fysshe and William Sergeaunt of the same, their heirs and assigns, a pyghtle called Teyntouryerd, formerly parcel of the Manor of Rychards Hall with a certain house built thereon called a "cherchhous sive a Gilde Halle" (as in No. III.) And they guarantee it to the aforesaid Henry, Robert, John, William, Thomas, William, Walter, John, John, Benedict, Thomas and William, their heirs and assigns, against all people. Witnesses:— John Barnard, John Fyssh, William Hert, John Pryour, Robert Gambown, John Baron, William Herne and others. Pakenham, 10 Dec: 2d Hen. VII.

3rd HENRY VII. (1488).

Robert Clerke and John Fysch of Pakenham give to William Gylle, John Herte, William Crysten, senior, and William Crysten, junior, of the same. Two acres of arable lying in Stalmerfeld between the land of William Crysten on the west, Robert Clerke on the east, abutting on a pitle of William Gylle on the north, and on the land of the said Robert on the south, their heirs and assigns. And Robert Clerke guarantees William Clerk against all people Witnesses:—William Crysten, Richard Wymbyl, Roger Calabyr and others. Dated at Pakenham 15 May, 3d Henry VII. since the Conquest of England.

7th HENRY VII. (1492).

I, Thomas Smyth of Walsham, give to Robert Cage of Pakenham, Katherine his wife, John Nunne of Drenxton, and John Hoo of Hetesett, their heirs and assigns, one half acre of mowable meadow lying in the meadow of Langham, next the meadow of Ixworth Priory on the south, and the meadow of the heirs of John Badwell on the north, one head abutting on the water course to the east, the other head abutting on the land late of John Carpenter called Canownnyshyll to the west, which aforesaid half acre I lately held conjointly with John Glovere of Stanton. Know ye also that I have appointed my beloved in Christ, John Hawys, junior, to deliver seisin &c. Dated at Langham 12 April in the 7th of Henry VII. since the Conquest. Sealed with a capital R. Witnesses:—Bartholomew Wymbyll, John Wymbyll, John Shukford, William Hawys, Robert Cook and others.

8th HENRY VII. (1492).

William Aubry and John Wade of Wolpet demise to John Goodson, Vicar of Pakenham, Robert Copenger of Wolpet, and Henry Cage of Pakenham, a piece of land estimated at half-an-acre, more or less, lying in the town of Wolpet in the field called Droveweye, between the land of the said John Goodson on the east, and the land late of Henry Creme on the west, abutting on the land of Richard Numan on the south, and of divers men on the north, which piece of land we held of the gift of Edward Seman, as more fully appears by a document from him to us [*no such document is to be found*]. Witnesses:—John Bawde, James Lane, Richard Numan, and others. Sealed at Wolpet the penultimate day of September in the 8th year of Henry the Seventh since the Conquest of England.

INDENTURE, 21st HENRY VII. (1505).

William Clerke, Richard Petyte, John Fyston, and William Fysh of Pakenham demise to Thomas Rose, sen., William Rose, Robert Sergeaunt, Robert Note, and George Ferwe of Thurston, three pieces of land lying diversely in the town and fields of Thurston. The first, estimated at one acre, lies in the field called Langlond, between the land late of John Roshebrok on the south, and that late of Thomas Becon on the north, abutting east on Medewewey, and west on Litilbussheweye. The second, estimated at three acres, lies in the same fields between the land of the aforesaid John Rosshebrok on the south, and that late of Edward Rose, now of John Bacon, on the north, abutting as the former piece. The third piece, estimated at seven roods, lies in the same field between the lands late of Edward Rose, now of John Bacon, on the south, and that of Nicholas Sergeaunt on the north, abutting as the former. These among other lands and tenements we held jointly with Robert Cage, now deceased, of the demise of George Tysoo, Chaplain, as appears more fully by a document dated the Octave of the Assumption in the eleventh year of Henry the Seventh since the Conquest of England [*no such document is known*].

The aforesaid Thomas Rose, William Rose, Robert Sergeaunt, Robert Note, and George Ferwe, their heirs and assigns, rendering to us our heirs and assigns three pence yearly at Michaelmas. And if it fall out that the said three pence of rent should be in arrear and not paid in any year at the said feast, in part or in whole, it shall be lawful to us, our heirs and assigns, to enter and distrain, and to take, remove, and retain the distresses till satisfaction is made with full arrearages. The one part of this indenture, sealed by us, to be retained by the aforesaid Thomas, William, Robert, Robert, and George, the other part, sealed by the above, to be retained by us. Witnesses:—Robert Rery, Vicar, George Tysoo, Chaplain, John Ferwe, George Rosshebrok, Thomas Becon, and others. Dated at Thurston 5 October, 8th of Henry VII., since the Conquest of England.

Four Seals, on one of which is a lion rampant.

COPY OF COURT ROLL, STANTON HALL, 3rd HENRY VIII. (15$\frac{11}{12}$).

John Perkyn, deceased, left to his wife, Margaret Perkyn, for life, and after her death to his executors, John Gryffyn and Robert Scott, one acre and half-a-rood of land lying between lands belonging to the town of Pakenham on the west, and abutting on Greystok Mille weye towards the south, which acre and half-rood they surrendered to the use of John Cage [*John Cage was Vicar of Pakenham from 1501 till his death in 1548*] and Robert Stokes, who are to pay yearly to the lord at the usual terms, twopence, one half-penny, one farthing, and one half-farthing.

5th HENRY VIII. (1514).

John Cage, son and heir of Katerine Cage, gives to John Hawys of Westrete in Walsham one acre and a-half of meadow lying in the meadow of Langham, next the meadow of Ixworth Priory on the south, and that of Richard Poley on the north, abutting on the water course towards the east, and on the land of John Carpenter, called Cannownyshell towards the west. This land came to him as heir of his mother the last feoffee, who had held it jointly with Robert Cage her husband, John Nunne of Drenxton, and John Hoo of Hesett of the gift, Thomas Smyth of Walsham, as more fully &c. [*no such document appears*]. Sealed at Langham 10 March, 5th Henry VIII., since the Conquest of England. Witnesses (endorsed):—John [*blank in orig.*], John Rocheman, John Fullere, William Grymesby, and many others.

6th HENRY VIII. (1515)

John Cage, son and heir of Katherine Cage, of Pakenham gives to Richard Cobdock and William Clerk, executors of Robert Cobdok, a close called Stalmer in the town and in the field of Pakenham called Grymstonfelde. And it is enclosed with hedges and ditches containing two acres. It lies between the lands of the manor of Bemannys on the south, and the land of William Fyston on the north. One head abuts on the land of the said town of Pakenham towards the west, and the other on the lands of divers men towards the east. Which close descended to me as heir to Katherine Cage my mother, the sole and last feoffee. She held, among other lands jointly with her husband, Robert Cage, Richard Reynghold of Wulfpett, and Robert Hoo of Hesett, on the demise of Robert Cage of Ratelysden, Henry Cage of Pakenham, Thomas Cage of Berdewell, and John Rossehebrok of Thurston, as more plainly &c. to the uses of the last will of Robert Cobdok, lately deceased. Sealed and dated at Pakenham 15 January, 6th of Henry VIII., since the Conquest of England. Endorsed, In the presence of John Cage, John Lyster, Ralph Wylton, and others.

INDENTURE, 6th HENRY VIII. (1515).

Richard Cobdok and William Clerk, Executors of Robert Cobdok, demise and by this indenture confirm to John Cage, his heirs, &c., one penny of yearly rent for a close called Stalmer *(as in previous deed)*, and if that penny be in arrear partly or wholly at the feast of St. Michael the Archangel it shall be lawful for the said John Cage, his heirs, &c., to distrain and to lead, drive, carry, and detain, and freely to dispose of the distraints, until &c. Richard Cobdok and William Clerk seal the part which John Cage is to keep, and *vice versâ*. Dated at Pakenham 15 January, 6th Henry VIII., since the Conquest of England.

A seal with a device resembling a ladder with two rungs.

6th HENRY VIII. (1514).

John Hawys of Westrete in Walsham demises to John Cage of Pakenham, John Skott of Walsham, and Thomas Reynberd of the same, half an acre of meadow in the meadow of Langham next the meadow of the Prior and Convent of Ixworth on the south, and the meadow of Richard Poley on the north; one head abuts on the water-course towards the east, the other on the land late of John Carpenter called Canownyshyll towards the west, which half-acre he had of the gift &c. of John Cage aforesaid, as appears &c. Dated at Langham 10 March 5th of Henry VIII., since the Conquest of England, to have &c. to the aforesaid John Cage, John Skott, and Robert Reynberd, their heirs &c. to the use of the aforesaid John Cage, his heirs &c. Dated at Langham 1 May, 6th Henry VIII., since the Conquest of England. Endorsed. Witnesses :—John Cotysins, John Rycheman, John Fullere, William Grymesby, and others.

Seal with a device, probably a merchant's mark.

7th HENRY VIII. (1516).

Richard Abell of Thurston, Benedict Fordham of Pakenham, John Bullok, John Lyenge, and John Abell of Thurston, give to Robert Sowter of Thurston, Richard Cobdok of Pakenham, Thomas Soper, Thomas Gambown, and John Lauerawns, four and a-half acres of arable, lying in two pieces in the town and fields of Pakenham. Whereof the first contains four acres in the field called Stonhyll between the land of John Lauerawns on the east, and of Thomas Sprynge on the west. One head abuts on the land of Thomas Sprynge and of John Lester towards the south, and the other head upon the way called "Ton wey" towards the north. The second piece contains half an acre and lies in the same field between the lands of the manor of the Convent of Saint Edmund on the east, and the land of the said John Lauerawns on the west. One head abuts on the land of the said John Lyster towards the south, and the other on the aforesaid way towards the north. Which two pieces of land among other lands and tenements we held of the demise of William Clerk, as appears by a document dated at Pakenham 5 January, 7th Henry VIII. (1515). To have and to hold &c. to the aforesaid &c. Dated at Pakenham 5 April, 7th Henry VIII. (1516). Witnesses:— John Cage, Vicar, William Clerk, Richard Wimbbyll, John Hunt, John Botown, and others.

8th HENRY VIII. (1516).

Know all men that I, Richard Abell of Thurston, have demised &c. to Robert Stokes of Pakenham, his heirs &c., all my right and claim, which I ever had or shall have, in two pieces of arable, containing four acres and a-half in the town and field of Pakenham. So that neither I, nor my heirs &c., should assert any right or claim in the aforesaid two pieces lying in the aforesaid town, and in the field called Stonhyll, or any parcel thereof. Guarantee to Robert Stokys [sic] against all people. Dated at Pakenham 13 May, 8th Henry VIII.

12th HENRY VIII. (1521).

John Barown of Pakenham demises to Edward Smyth, William Clerk, Thomas Cage, John Lystere, John Boxe, Robert Stokys, Thomas Broke, Thomas Crysten, Ralph Wylton, William Fyston, Robert Sygo, Thomas Fordham, Robert Serjawnt, and John Serjawnt of Pakenham, two acres of arable lying in the town of Pakenham in the field called Stalmerfeld, between the land late of William Crysten on the west, and the land late of Robert Clerk on the east. It abuts towards the north on a pightle late William Gylle, and towards the south on the land of the said Robert Clerk. Which two acres we formerly held with John Goodsone, some time Vicar, Henry Cage, John Roschebrok, Robert Cage, William Hert, Richard Abell, Roger Calabyr, John Fyston, William Crysten of Grymston, William Serjawnt, John Roos, William fysch, and Ralph Fysch, them lately deceased, of the demise of John Hert, William Crysten, as by a document of the penultiman day of March in the 8th year of Henry VIII. since the Conquest of England more plainly appears. To have and to hold &c. Sealed and dated at Pakenham 29th January, 12th Henry VIII. since the Conquest of England (1519). Witnesses:—John Cage, Vicar, William Dencrosse, John Pecok, Henry Brook, John Halle, Robert Box, and others.

21st HENRY VIII. (1529).

William Clerk, junior, of Pakynham, John Nell, and John Botown demise to Edward Smyth of Pakynham, yoman, Thomas Cage, Thomas Cristyn, John Lawrens, *alias* John Smyth, John Baron, senior, Robert Sargaunt, John Sargaunt, Robert Sigo, John Boxe, Thomas Gambon,

Richard Cobdok, John Lister, weaver, and Thomas Lister, weaver, of the same, two pieces of land lying separately in the town and fields of Pakynham, whereof one piece is estimated at one acre, and lies between the land of Bury Abbey in the occupation of me the aforesaid William Clerk on the west, and the land of me the said John Nell on the east, and it abuts towards the south on a way called Bery wey, aud towards the north on the land of the said Convent. And the other piece lies in the field called Akedale, between the lands of John Baron on both sides, and it abuts towards the east on the land of the same, and towards the west on the land of the vicar of Pakynham, which two pieces, among others, we held along with Isabella Wymbill, late of Pakynham, widow, now deceased, of the demise of William Clerk, senior, of Bury St Edmunds, Ben Clerk of Stowlangtoft, John Lister of Pakynham, and the said Richard Cobdok, as is more fully contained in a feoffment made by us, and dated at Pakynham on the 8th May in the 18th year of Henry VIII. To have and to hold &c. Sealed and dated at Pakynham 13 July, 21st Henry VIII. First endorsement *(cancelled)*:— In the presence of John Cage, Vicar, William Fyston, Thomas Syer, Edward Tomys, and others; 14 September, year and place within written. Second endorsement:—In the presence of William Calabyr, John Calabyr, Henry Brook, Simund Cage, Thomas Wylton, and others; 14 September, year and place within written.

21st Henry VIII. (1529).

Richard Cobdok and William Clerk, executors of Robert Cobdok late of Pakynham, give to Edward Smyth, yoman, Thomas Cage, Thomas Crystyn, John Lawrens, *alias* John Smyth, John Baron, senior, Robert Sergant, John Sergant, Christopher(?) Sligo, John Boxe, Thomas Gambon, John Hert, John Lister, senior, and Thomas Lister, wever, all of Pakynham, a close called Stalmere, and a piece of meadow lying in towns and fields of Pakynham aforesaid, and of Langham in the county of Suffolk. Which close contains two acres, and is enclosed with hedges and ditches, and lies in Grymstonfeld, between the land of Bemannys Manor on the south, and the land of William Fyston on the north, abutting towards the east on the lands of divers men, and towards the west on that of the said town of Pakynham. And the aforesaid piece of meadow is estimated at half an acre, and lies in the meadow of the said town of Langham next that of Ixworth Priory on the south, and of Robert Poleye on the north, abutting towards the east on the watercourse, and towards the west on the land of John Carpenter, called Canownyshill. Which close and meadow we held of the gift of John Cage, late of Pakynham, son and heir of Katerine Cage, John Skott of Walsham and Thomas Reynberd of the same, as in two documents &c., dated, Pakynham and Langham, the 15th and the 16th January, 6th Henry VIII., to the service, use, and profit of the town of Pakynham for ever. Dated at Pakyhham 13th July, 21th Henry VIII. T. Clerk *(with a paraphe like a pair of scissors)*. State and Seisin delivered 14 September same year. Witnesses:—John Cage, Vicar, William Fyston, Thomas Syer, Edward Tomys, and others.

21st HENRY VIII. (1529).

Thomas Cage, John Lyster, Thomas Fordham, and Robert Sargant demise to Edward Smyth, yoman, Thomas Cristyn, John Lawrens *alias* John Smyth, John Baron, senior, John Sargant, Robert Sigo, John Boxe, Thomas Gambon, Richard Cobdok, and Thomas Lister, wever, all of Pakynham, a piece of land containing four acres lying in the field called Hardale of Pakynham, between the lands of Bury Monastery on either part, and abutting eastward on a path called Malguysmere, and westward on a way called Thetfordwey, which piece of land is estimated at four acres, more or less, and which we held conjointly with Robert Stokys late of Pakynham, now deceased, of the gift of Nicholas Abell late of Thurston, Benedict Fordham late of Pakenham, John Bullok, John Lynge, and John Abell late of Thurston, as contained in document made by us, dated at Pakynham 27 April, 18th Henry VIII., for service use, and profit of the town of Pakynham according to the tenor of the will of the above-named Robert Stokes. Dated at Pakynham 13 July, 21st Henry VIII. T. Clerk *(paraphe as before)*. State and Seisin delivered 14 September, same year and place. Witnesses:—William Calabyr, John Calabyr, Henry Brook, William Brook, Symond Cage, Thomas Wylton, and others.

EXTRACTS FROM COPY OF COPY OF ROBERT STOKES' WILL, made 26 March 1525 in Town Estate Trustees' box :—

"Item : I give & bequeath to yͤ Church & to yͤ Town of Pakenham a Close of 4 acres Inclosed lying at Stonhill and 4 acres at Hardale, & an half acre at Stonhill to that intent to keep mine Obitday yearly during for ever under this Form. That is to say 4ᵈ to yͤ Clerk to say Dirige, 4ᵈ to yͤ Ringers and 4ᵈ to Poor Folk. And yͤ residue of yͤ profit of yͤ said Land to be used to yͤ profit of yͤ said Church of Pakenham." By a subsequent provision he leaves on certain contingencies half of "the tenement that I died in" to the Church of Pakenham. Witnesses :—John Cage, Vicar, John Lester, John Cobdock, with others.

This will contains the only trace of so-called "superstitious uses," and probably escaped the spoilers' hands owing to its smallness, or to its being included in the feoffment of 1538.

21st HENRY VIII. (1529).

Thomas Cage, John Lister, and Thomas Fordham demise to Edmund Smyth, yoman, Thomas Cristyn, John Lawrens *alias* John Smyth, John Baron, senior, Robert Sargant, John Sargant, Robert Sigo, John Boxe, Thomas Gambon, Richard Cobdok, and Thomas Lister, all of Pakynham, two pieces of land in the town and fields of Pakynham, whereof one piece, estimated at four acres, lies in the field called Stonhill, between the lands of the said John Lawrens on the east, and the lands of Thomas Sprynge on the west, abutting southward on the land of the same Thomas Sprynge, and the land of me the said John Lister, and northward on the way called "Le Town Wey." And the other piece is estimated at half an acre, and lies in the same field between the land of the manor of Bury Abbey on the east, and the land

60

of me the said John Lawrens on the west, abutting southward on the
land of me the said John Lister and northward on the said way called
"Le Ton Weye." Which two pieces of land we held conjointly with
Robert Stokes late of Pakynham, and Ralph Wilton, now deceased, of
the gift of Robert Sowter late of Thurston, Nicholas Cobdok, Thomas
Soper, Thomas Gambon, and John Lawrens, as more fully &c., dated at
Pakenham 13 May, 8th Henry VIII. To have and to hold &c. to the
service, use, and profit of the town of Pakynham according to the tenour
of the Will of Robert Stokes. Dated 13 July, 21st Henry VIII.
T. Clerk (paraphe as before). Endorsed: State and Seisin delivered in
the presence of William Calabyr, John Calabyr, Henry Brook, Simond
Cage, Thomas Wylton, and others, 14 September, same year and place.

Fragment of seal, with a rude representation of a bird-cage.

28th HENRY VIII. (1537).

Edmund Smyth, Thomas Cage, Thomas Crysten, John Lauerans
alias John Smyth, John Barown, senior, Robert Serjawnt, John Serjawnt,
Robert Sygo, Richard Cobdok, and Thomas Lister, sengilman, all of
Pakenham, give to John Lister of Pakenham aforesaid, wever, two
pieces of land lying diversely in the town and fields of Pakenham, of
which one piece is estimated at one acre, and lies between the land of
Bury Abbey lately in the occupation of William Clerk on the west, and
the land of John Neel on the east, abutting southward on the way
called "Bury weye," and northward on the land of the said Abbey.
The second piece of land is estimated at one acre, and lies in the same
parish in the field called Akedale, between the lands of John Barown on
either part, and abutting eastward on the land of the said John Barown,
and westward on the land of the Vicarage of Pakenham, which two
pieces we lately held conjointly with John Box and Thomas Gambown
lately deceased, of the demise of William Clerk, junior, John Neel, and
John Botown of Pakenham as is more fully contained &c., dated 13
July, 21st Henry VIII. Moreover the aforesaid John Lester acquired
the said two pieces for a certain sum of money of the aforesaid Edmund
Smyth, Thomas Cage, and the rest above written in the name of the
town of Pakenham. To have and to hold &c. Dated at Pakenham
9 April, 28th Henry VIII., after the Conquest of England. Endorsed:
State and Seisin delivered the day and place within written in the
presence of John Cage, Ralph Mas . all, Robert Bele, Richard Feryars,
John Guma . ., and others.

20th September, 16th CHARLES I.

Indenture written on bad parchment with worse ink, but, so far as
can be made out, to the same uses as by Feoffment of 1538 *(page 68).*

20th January 1651 (o.s.).

Indenture made the fower & twentie day of January in the yeare of
our Lord god according to the computation of the Church of England
one thousand six hundred fifty and one Between Edmund Humphry

the elder of Pakenham geñ and John Cooke of great Horningsherth geñ sonne and heire of John Cooke late of Pakenham geñ, deceased of the one part, and Sir William Spring Barronett, Henry Bright geñ, William Bright sonne of the sayd Henry Bright, Zachary Catlyne clarke, Richard Cooke geñ, William Cooke his sonne, Roger Cooke geñ, John Cooke, Richard Cooke, Ralfe Cooke sonnes of the sayd Roger Cooke, Edmund Humfry sonne of the sayd Edmund Humfry the elder, John Clarke, Richard Clarke sonne of the sayd John Clarke, Clement Gilly, John Towler the elder, John Towler sonne of the sayd John Towler, Xtopher Towler, William Towler sonne of the sayd Xtopher, Robᵗ Blumfeild the elder, Robᵗ Blumfeild sonne of the sayd Robᵗ Blumfeild, Nathaniell Jorden, William Parker, Henry Stegell, William Best, Robᵗ Pettit, Edmond Blumfeild John Sculford, & John Brooke, Inhabitants and owners of land, or Heires of dᵒ in Pakenham of thother pᵗᵉ **Whereas** Sʳ Robert Gardenar late of Pakenham Knight bequeathed Forty Pounds to be laid out in land towards the releife & mayntenance of the poore people of Pakenham for ever **And Whereas** certaine of the inhabitants of Pakenham had received of John Webb Esq̃, Executor, the sᵈ fortypounds, & with it bought of John Hasell late of Watsfeild, yeoman, & John Burlingham late of Wattesfeild aforesᵈ, yeoman, **All that Closse** of pasture called Goore's, containing by estimacion Six Acres, more or less, in Stanton, between the lands late of Sʳ Thomas Jermyn Knᵗ, & now of the younger sonnes of Sʳ Arthur Cordell Knᵗ & Barronᵗ deceased in pᵗᵉ, & the lands of the Manor of Northall in pᵗᵉ on the South pᵗᵉ, & a Comõn way leading from Stanton to Wattsfeild aforesᵈ on the North pᵗᵉ and abutting on the same highway towards the East, together with &c. And conveyed the same to Sʳ William Spring of Pakenham, Knᵗ, John Cooke the elder of the same towne geñ the aforesayd Edmund Humfry & John Cooke, Peter Sergeant, & William Prior by Indenture of March 13 in the 21ˢᵗ year of James, King of England **And Whereas** the sᵈ Sir Willm Spring, &c. are all dead, so that Edmund Humfry & John Cooke do only survive **Now to the Intent** that the guift of Sir Robᵗ Gardener may be continued **Witnesseth this Indenture** that the sayd Edmund Humfry & John Cooke **Have bargained**, sold &c. unto the sayd Sʳ William Springe, Henry Bright, William Bright, Zachary Catlyn, Richard Cooke, William Cooke, Roger Cooke, John Cooke, Richard Cooke, Ralfe Cooke, Edmund Humfry the sonne, John Clarke, Richard Clarke, Clement Gilly, John Towler the elder, John Towler his sonne, Xtopher Towler, Willm Towler, Robᵗ Blumfeild thelder, Robᵗ Blumfeild his sonne, Nathaniell Jorden, Willm Parker, Henry Stegell, Willm Best, Robᵗ Pettit, Edmund Blumfeild, John Scullford, and John Brooke their heires & assigns **All the** aforesᵈ closse &c. **To have and to hold** the sayd closse &c. **Upon this trust** &c. that the rents &c. be disposed of for & towards the releife of the poore people of Pakenham in such manner as the Churchwardens & Overseers, or the greater number of them shall think fitt **And** upon further trust that when the above feoffees are by death or departure reduced to two, those two shall upon the reasonable request, and costs and charges of the then inhabitants & Landholders in the sᵈ pish shall convey &c. to such a competent number of inhabitants & owners as shall be thought fitt to such intents &c. **And the sayd** Edmund Humfry &c. do them the

sayd Sr William Springe &c. Edmund Blomefield &c. warrant &
defend for ever **And the sayd** John Cooke &c. do them the sayd
Sr William Springe &c. Robt Blumefeild Edmond Blomefeild &c.
warrant & defend for ever. **In witness** whereof &c.

Edmund Humphrey.   John Cooke.

Seal.   *Seal gone.*

17 December, 9th William III. (1697)

Indenture made 17 December, 9th of William III. (1697), between
William Towler, Knacker, of the one parte And Hamond Lestrange the
elder Esq̃, Hamond Lestrange the younger, gent̃, John Cooke gent̃,
John Towler the elder, John Towler the younger, Nathaniell Jurden,
Joseph Sparke, John Manistree, John Sculthorpe, Ralph Lloyd, Henry
Sharpe the younger, George Codd, Abraham Jurden and John Spensley
of the other p^te **Witnesseth** that the s^d William Towler for the sum
of five shillings paid by the s^d Hamond Lestrange &c. **hath** granted to
&c. all and singuler the &c. in Pakenham, Stanton, Badwell Ash,
Elmeswell, Woolpit and Thurston, or elsewhere, lately had to them
& their heirs of William Towler, late of Ixworth, Knacker, and Phillip
Palfrey of the same town, yeoman, both since dead, &c. **To Have
& to Hold** &c. to be paid and laid out towards [*some words perished*]
Tenths & Fifteenths And other Taxes hereafter to be imposed in and
upon the Town of Pakenham afores^d [*some words perished*] and all
other Charges of the same Town for ever The ancient rents &
services &c.

(Signed) Wile: Towler.

Seal (a bust in profile).

Schedule attached of all messuages, &c. intended to be conveyed by
the above Indenture :—

PAKENHAM.

One Messuage now devided into severall dwellings for the poore
called Guildhall now or late in the severall occupations of John Crisp,
the widd^w Vintcent And the widd^w Sego the widd^w Copin with the
yarde adjoyning sometimes called Taynter row yard or pitle sometime
parcel of the Man^r of Richard's Hall in pakenham contayning in length
on the south p^te sixteen roods And in length on the North p^te Eleven
roods And in breadth towards the East head four roods and two foot
And in breadth towards the west head nine roods four foot. **One**
shope outhouse or storehouse Abutting upon Bridg street in pakenham
towards the North And sideth upon the Messuages & Tenem^ts of Henry
Sharp as well east as west in the occupaton of John Brooke. **Half** An
acre of arrable land lying in Norman's Close the East head abbutteth
upon A close called Green Coake and sideth upon the lands of Henry
Sharp towards the South And the Lands of Mr John Spensley within-
named towards the North in the occupaton of Nathaniell Jordan J^n

Two Acres of arrable land lying in little Brome the East head abutteth upon the Lands of Sr Thomas Spring lord of the Mann^r and sideth upon the lands of Sr Thos Spring on the North, and the same of Mr Spensley on the south p^{te} **Two** peices of Arrable land adjoyning the North head abutteth upon Tunnway and sideth upon the Lands of the L^d of the Mann^r towards the west And the lands of Mr Spensley towards the East in the occupaton of Nathanniell Jurden **Halfe** an Acre of land called St Edmonds headlong abutteth upon Tunnway towards the South and sideth upon the gleab land belonging to the vicarage of Pakenham towards the West and divers men towards the East now or late in the occupation of Nathaniell Jordan **One** pasture Close contayning four acres called Taylors Close abutteth upon Tunnway towards the North in a feild called Edgfeild in the occupaton of Hamond Lestrang Esq **One** Acre of arable land at Gayford Hill abutteth upon Brandon way towards the West and sideth upon the land of John Towler toward the South and the Lands of Henry Sharp towards the North in the occupaton of Nathaniell Jordan Jⁿ **One** peice more theire conteyning four Acrces the West head abutteth upon Brandon way and sideth upon the lands of Thomas Bright Esq on the South and the lands of Sr Thomas Spring on the North and Maulings Mere towards the East in the occupaton of Nathan^{ll} Jordan **One** three roods of Land more theire Abutteth upon Maulings path towards the East and sideth upon the Lands of Sr Thomas Spring towards the South And the Lands of John Jaskin towards the North. **One** acre of arrable land in highfeild the East head abutteth upon the great road called Bury-way leading from Ixworth to Bury And sideth upon John Jaskin towards the North And sideth upon the Lands of the Widd^w Tomson towards the South in the occupaton of Nathaniell Jordan Jun **One** peice contayning three roods lying in preists meadow abutteth upon the River towards the North And Sideth upon the lands of Henry Sharp towards the West and the lands of John Jaskin towards the West. **One** close of pasture contayning three roods the East head abutteth the land of Sr Thomas Spring And sideth upon Stow Lane towards the South in the occupaton of Nathaniell Jordan **One** other peice of arrable land lying at a place called windhill conteyning four Acres the East head abutteth upon the Lands of Malkins-hall And upon the Lands of Malkins-hall afores^d towards the South And the Lands of Malkins-hall in part And the lands of Abraham Jordan in parte towards the North in the occupaton of William Evett **One** Acrce of Arrable Land lying inclosed the East head abutteth upon the Lands of Ann Lany widd^w called Reeves and sideth upon the Lands of the s^d Ann Lany towards the North and the Lands of Sr Simond Dewes towards the South in the occupaton of William Evett. **One** close conteyning Two Acres more or less in a place called Backfeild the South head abutteth upon the Town land of Pakenham and sideth upon the Lands of the s^d Mrs Lany towards the East and the lands of Edmond Baxter called Stamers towards the West in the occupaton of Robt Barrett **One** other close conteyning Two Acres the South head abutteth upon the Town land of pakenham towards the South and sideth upon the Lands of John Clarke towards the West the North head abutteth upon the Lands of John Clarke in the occupaton of Edward Hatfield Alias Mayor

One piece of Arrable land lying in Backfeild conteyning five acres the South head abutteth upon the Land of John Clarke and the North head abutteth upon the Lands of Edmond Baxter and sideth upon the lands of Hamond Le Strange Esq̃ towards the East in the occupaton of Robᵗ Barrett.

Badwell Ash.

One piece of Meadow conteyning one Acre lying in the Lamos Meadow the North head abutteth upon the River And sideth towards the East upon the Lands of William [*blank*] Esq̃ and upon the West one the Lands of William May in the occupaton of John Gilfird.

Langham.

One piece of Meadow conteyning halfe an Acre abutteth upon the River aforesᵈ towards the South and sideth upon John Rainbird towards the East And the Lands of Mʳ William Syer towards the West in the occupaton of John Gilfird.

Stanton.

One Close called Goores conteyning Six Acres more or less the North side lyeth upon the way leading from Stanton to Wattisfeild the East head abutteth upon the same way and sideth upon the Lands of Mʳ Caple towards the South in the occupaton of Giles Rust   **One** other Close conteyning two Acres and three roodes the South head abutteth upon Hawthorpe way and sideth upon the lands of Mʳ Caple towards the East the North head abutteth upon Hoggs wood in the occupaton of Giles Rust   **One** other Close conteyning one acre and halfe A roode abutteth upon Hawthorpe towards the South and sideth upon pakenham Close towards the East And sideth upon Mʳ Caple towards the West and abutteth upon Hoggswood towards the North in the occupaton of Giles Rust.

Thurston.

One Close conteyning one Acre the West head abutteth upon Meadowway And sideth upon the Lands of Roger Kerington Esq̃ towards the South and sideth upon the Lands of Robᵗ Cheenery towards the North in the occupation of George Blackborne   **One** other Close conteyning five Acres sideth upon Stocknow Green towards the North and abutteth upon the Land of George Blackborne towards the West & sideth upon the Land of Mʳ Blackborne And Mʳ Gibb in pᵗᵉ towards the South in the occupaton of George Blackborne.

Elmeswell.

One meadow called pakenham meadow the East head abutteth upon the Lane leading from Elmeswell Church towards Woolpitt upon Newbridge Alias Nunsbridge and sideth upon the Land of Mʳ Houghton towards the South And the Lands of the Widdʷ Magar towards the North in the occupaton of Thomas Osbourn.

65

Endorsed: State and seisin, &c., John Brownsmith Vic̃, Nathaniel Mathew. Sealed and delivered, being, &c., John Wright, Sutton Jo: Cony. Wiłłm Towler, Hamon L'Estrange Esq̃ and oʳˢ, Feoffmᵗ of Pakenham.—Pakenham Feoffmᵗ 1697.

20 June 1741.

Hamon L'Estrange of Bury Sᵗ Edmunds Esq̃ and Henry Sharpe of Ixworth, Woolcomber (surviving feoffees), hand on the estate, but with the shope or outhouse, "wasted," to Thomas Matthew of Pakenham Yeoman, of the second part and William Hollingworth Esq̃, William Hollingworth his son, Rev. James Challis, Vicar, Rev. Harvey Aspin, Rev. Benjamin Lany, Edmund Manistre, Robert Manistre his son, William Lord, and Nathaniel Lord his son, John Barker, Edmund Copping, Clothier, and Thomas Copping his son, Nathaniel Gilson the younger, William Doe, and Samuel Lusher. **Upon trust** (reasonable reparations deducted) "**First** to and for the reparations of the Church of the said Parish of Pakenham, next for and towards other Common Town Charges of the said Parish and the residue for and towards the maintenance of the poore of the said Parish." Roger Boldero of Ixworth Gent̃ is appointed Attorney.

HAMON L'ESTRANGE.   HENRY SHARPE.

Seal.   *Seal.*

(A Blackamoor's head in profile in both cases).

Endorsed: Hamon L'Estrange & oʳˢ, Captain Hollingworth & oʳˢ, Feoffment of Pakenham Town Land. Sealed and delivered (being &c.) by Hamon L'Estrange. Witnesses :—Robert Wakefield, Geo: Boldero. Sealed and delivered (being &c.) by Henry Sharpe. Witnesses :—John Andrews, Geo: Boldero. State and seizin, day and year first written, had by Roger Boldero, and immediately delivered to Thomas Mathew. Witnesses :—Abra: Mathew, Geo: Boldero.

51st GEORGE III., 1811.

Indenture of four parts between William Manistre of Lainson, Essex, farmer, eldest son and heir of Robert Manistre, late of Cockfield, Suffolk, farmer, who was only son and heir of Edmund Manistre, late of Pakenham, Suffolk, surviving feoffee of feoffment of 20 June 1741, of the first part, Gill Stedman of Pakenham, gentleman, of the second part, George, Lord Calthorpe, John Spring Casborne of Pakenham, clerk, Walter John Spring Casborne his son, John Foster, son of Gill Stedman, Robert Jannings, farmer, and Robert his son, Dennis Chandler, farmer, and Dennis his son, Robert Langham, butcher, and Robert his son, Edmund Jacob, farmer, and John his son, and William Carpenter Ray, Vicar of Pakenham, of the third part, William Golding, innholder, of the fourth part, reciting feoffment of 1741, and recording exchanges made in Pakenham under Enclosure Act of 42nd George III. (enrolled 12 February 1805), William Manistre grants &c. to the said Lord Calthorpe &c. all the &c. upon Trusts (reasonable repairs excepted), first for the reparations of the Church of Pakenham, next for the Common Town Charges, and the residue for the maintenance of the poor.

55th GEORGE III.

Hepworth Enclosure Act allots lands in Hepworth in exchange for lands in Stanton and Hepworth.

58th GEORGE III.

Walsham-le-Willows Enclosure Act allots lands in exchange for lands therein described.

In 1820 1 acre 2 rods in Langham and Badwell Ash are exchanged for 2 acres 12 rods 6 perch in Hepworth adjoining the 20 acres already held there.

The income was expended, as appears by the churchwardens' books, in repairs of the Church and other Common Town Charges, such as building a bridge, paying a schoolmaster, vaccinating children, paying for militia substitutes, and in allowing old people to live rent free in the Workhouse or Guildhall. The Parliamentary Charity Commissioners report that in 1822 a petition was presented to the Court of Chancery stating (very inaccurately as appears from the above) that the whole income had for some years past been applied towards the repairs of the church, and asking for a new scheme. This was ordered on the 6th of April 1826, providing that the income of the lands, which were guessed at as being Stokes' gift, should go towards church repairs and the rest towards poor people belonging to the parish of Pakenham who did not receive parochial relief, such people to be selected by the trustees, or the major part of them, at their discretion. The Commissioners recommended that in view of the small number not in receipt of parish relief, such industrious and necessitous persons as these should first be relieved, next such as received only occasional parish relief, as the Trustees thought proper, the balance to be applied for the benefit of any other poor persons whom the Trustees should select, provided that it should not be done in lieu of parish relief. These recommendations were never adopted, and the charities were distributed under the order of 1826 until the year 1863, when a new scheme was sent down by the Charity Commissioners, joining the supposed Stokes' gift with the Town Estate again, and dividing the income into three equal parts, one for the church, one for education, and the third for selling coal or clothing at a cheap rate, or for a penny bank, or, in effect, for almost anything of like nature which the Trustees might think desirable. At the same time the requirements of belonging to the parish and of not receiving parish relief were removed. The Rev. Charles W. Jones, Vicar, Robert Stedman and G. W. Mathew, churchwardens, the Rev. Walter John Spring Casborne, clerk, the Rev. Charles Jones, clerk, late Vicar, James Jannings, farmer, and Frederic Gough, Lord Calthorpe, were constituted Trustees, the Vicar and Churchwardens to be Trustees *ex officio*, vacancies of the other Trusteeships to be filled by co-optation subject to approval by the Charity Commissioners. In 1884 a fresh order was made, placing all the parish charities, viz: Cook's, Bright's, and the Poor's Estate or Poor's Firing, under the same management as the Town Estate and Stutter's Charity, *i.e.*, the Vicar and Churchwardens being *ex officio* Trustees and the Rev. Prebendary

Harry Jones, Thomas Thornhill, Esq, M.P., Henry Outlaw, farmer, Alfred Peck, thatcher, and Dennis Burton, beershop keeper, being non-official trustees. Non-official vacancies to be filled up by the parishioners at a parish meeting. In 1897, in accordance with the Local Government Act 1894, the non-ecclesiastical charities were again separated from the Town Estate, which last remains as before.

Pakenham Town Estate.

FEOFFMENT OF 1538, 30th HENRY VIII.

KNOW all men that be present and they that this **Dede** hereafter shall **Rede or Here that we** Edmund Smyth Thomas Crysten William Fysoon Thomas Cage Edward Parker Henry Petyt of Pakenam in the Countie of Suffolk yemen and John Lawrance alias Smyth wever Edward Broke carpenter John Lyster wever in the countie aforesaid at the Special Request and Instance as well of Edward Parker and Thomas Pecok Churche wardens of Pakenam aforeseyd as at the request & instance & by the assent & consent of all the inhabytants & paryssheners of the seyd town off Pakenam **Have Gyvyn** and granted and by this oure present wrytyng have confirmyd to John Cage Clerke vycar off Pakenam aforeseid all our londys & tenements rentys services woods underwoods Hegges & Rowys wayes pathes and fedynges with all every & synguler ther appertaining Sette lying & beying in the towne & fyldys of Pakenam thurston langgam Hasshfeld parva wolpet elmeswell & stanton or elswhere within the countie of Suff which londys & tenements with the premisses have ben namyd & at this present bene towne londs of Pakenam aforseid of the whyche londs tenements & other the premisses **We the** aforseid Edmund Smyth Thomas Crysten william Fyston Thomas Cage Edward Parker & Henry Petit John Lawrence alias Smyth Edward Broke & John lyster at this present stond & ben sesid dystyncle & severally Symply & without ony condycion to us & to oure heires of the gyfte grante & confirmacyon of dyvers men whose namys Successively followyth **Fyrst** of a pece of medow conteyning halfe a Aker in the medow of langm nere the medow late suppressed Pryory of yxworth on the southe syde & ye medow of Robard Polye on ye northe ye est hed abuttyng on ye water cours & the west hed on the lond of John Carpenter the whyche halfe Aker with the appurtenances lying as afore is rehersid I the fore namyd Edmund lately had of the gyfte grante & confirmacion of Thomas Cage Thomas Crysten John Laurence John barnes the elder Robard Sergiant John Sergyant Robt Sygo and Thomas Lyster as by there dede Datyd the xxviij day of Apryll aᵒ R: R: Henricy viij xxviij more playnly doth apere **And** of one other pece of medow extemyd for one Aker lying in litle Hasshefeld in the grete medow at Londherst other wysse cawlyd mykyl medow be twen the medow of ye late suppressed pryory of yxworth ageynst ye northe & ye medow of the manor of hasshefeld aforseyd ageynst the South the est abuttyng on the medow of dyvers men & ye west hed upon the comen

68

Ryver yᵉ whyche aker of medow I the seid Edmund Smyth had of the gifte grants & confirmacyon of John lister willyam fiston Thomas Cristen John Cage Thomas Cage Thomas Broke William Calabor John Nelle Richard Cobdok Henricus Cobdok John barn & John Laurence as by ther dede datyd yᵉ xxviij day of Apryll anᵒ R: R: henricj viij xxᵗⁱ viijᵐᵒ yᵉ yer aforseid more playnli aperith **And** a pece of medow cōteynyng one aker lying in the towne & fylds of wollpeth & Elmeswell **And** one pece of pasture contᵍ iij Rods lying betwen wolpett & Drynkston Nordolleweye ageynst the Souths the one hed abuttyng upon the lond of Thomas hart yᵉ whyche pece of medow & pasture with yᵉ appurtenances I yᵉ said John Smyth lately had of the gifte grant and confirmacyon off William Clerke Robᵗ Cage Thomas Soper William Calabor John barn & benet Boxxe as by ther ded datyd the xxvii off aprill anᵒ R: Rs Henryci viij xxviij playnlye aperith **Also** iiij pecs of lond yᵉ fyrst cawlid Stallmere lond conteynyng by estymacyon iiij acres of lond betwen the lond late william Fysshe of the est & yᵉ lond of yᵉ aforeseid william Fyston on the west yᵉ north hed abuttyng on the close of yᵉ seid william fiston the second pece contᵍ iij Rods lying betwen yᵉ londys of yᵉ seid Thomas Cristen on yᵉ southe & yᵉ fore acrs aforseid ageynst yᵉ northe yᵉ one head abuttith on the londs of the house of bury yᵉ iij pece contᵍ iij rods lying nere Fowle Slow between yᵉ londs of yᵉ seid House or monestery of bury of bothe part yᵉ west hed abutteth on rychard Hall lond & yᵉ est hed abutteth on yᵉ lond late Roger Strange yᵉ fort pece inclosid contᵍ iij Rods lying in Pakenam aforseid nere fowle Slow wey yᵉ est hed abutts on yᵉ lond of Richard Haull yᵉ whyche fower pecs with the appurtenances we yᵉ forseid Thomas Cryston & william Fiston lately had to us & our heres of the gifte grant & confirmacyon of William Clerke Robard Cage Thomas lyster Thomas Sopor William Calabor John barn yᵉ yonger benet Box as by ther ded datid at Pakanam yᵉ xxvj day of April anno R: R: Henrici viijᵛⁱ xxviijᵛᵒ more playnli aperith **And** one close cawlid Stawllmere contˢ ij acrs as with dyches & heggs it lythe inclosid lying in the feld of Pakenam cawlid grynston Fyld betwen the londs of yᵉ maner of bemans of the southe & yᵉ londs of william fyston ageynst yᵉ north yᵉ est hed abutting on yᵉ londs of dyvers men yᵉ whyche Close with yᵉ appurtenances I yᵉ seid William Fiston lateli to me & my heyers of yᵉ gifte grant & confirmacyon of Edmund Smyth Thomas Cage Thomas Crysten John barn yᵉ elder Robᵗ Sergyant John Sergiant Robᵗ Sygo John lyster & Thomas lyster as by ther Dede dattyd at Pakeman yᵉ viij day of aprill anno R: R: Henricy viijᵛⁱ xxviijᵛᵒ planelyer aperith **Also** ij pecs of lond whereof yᵉ fyrst lying in thurston contᵍ by estymacyon fyve acrs of lond & lyght nere yᵉ lond of yᵉ monestery of bury & yᵉ londs of John Drury in pᵗ ageynst yᵉ southe & yᵉ comen way cawlyd Stokk (?) grene ageynst yᵉ northe yᵉ est hed abutting on yᵉ londs of yᵉ sayde monestery & yᵉ west hed on yᵉ lond of yᵉ seid John Drury the other pece lyght in lower Stanston contᵍ ij acr & iij rods nere the londs of sir Thomas Jermen knyght ageynst yᵉ est & yᵉ londs of John Spryng caulyd Rusall lond ageynst yᵉ west yᵉ north hed abutteth on Hoggswoode & yᵉ lond of yᵉ seid Sʳ Thomas in parte & yᵉ Southe head upon Hawshore waye yᵉ whyche ij pecs of lond wᵗ thapp-tenncs we yᵉ forseid Thomas Cage & williã fyston lately had to us & our heyers of yᵉ gyft grante & confirmacⁿ of williã clerke yᵉ sone of willyam clerke Rob.t Cage y.e son of Thomas Cage Thomas Lyster thomas Sopor John barn y.e yonger & benet box as by ther dede datyd at thurston y.e xxvj day of Apryll anno R: R: Henricy viij xxviij more playnely aperith **And** a pece of medow & lond y.e medow lying in Pakenam cont.g iij Rods nere y.e medow of y.e monestery ageynst y.e northe & y.e medow of y.e suppressed priori of yxwurthe ageynst y.e southe y.e est hed abuttyng on y.e ryver & y.e west hed on y.e medow of y.e forseid monestery y.e pece of lond conteynyth iij Rods lying in thurston aforseid nere y.e lond of John prior ageynst y.e northe y.e west hed abutting on y.e comen waye y.e whyche ij pecs of medow & lond we y.e forseid Thomas Cage & William Fyston lateli has to us & oure heres of the gyft grant & confirma͠cn of William Clerk Robard Cage Thomas lyster Thomas Soper Thoms [*cancelled*] John barn y.e yonger Benet Box John Cage vicar of pakenam as by ther dede datyd y.e xxvj day of Aprill anno Regni Regis Henrici viij xxviij more plainli aperith **And** of ij pecs of lond wherof y.e fyrst is extemyd for iiij akers lying in Stonyhill Feld betwen y.e lond of y.e seid John Lawrence of y.e est & y.e lond late Thomas Sprynge ageynst y.e west y.e sowthe hede abuttyng on y.e lond of y.e seid thomas Sprynge & y.e lond of John Lyster y.e northe hed abutting on y.e towne weye y.e ij pece extemyd for half acre lying in y.e same feld betwen y.e manor lond of y.e monestery of bury ageynst y.e est & y.e lond of y.e seid John Laurence ageynst y.e west y.e south hed abuttyng on y.e lond of y.e seid John Lyster & y.e northe hed upon y.e seid towne waye y.e whyche pece of lond with thapptenn͠cs I y.e forseid Edward Parker lately had to me & myn heres of y.e gyfte grante & confirma͠cn of Edmund Smyth Thomas Cristen John Laurence alias Smyth John Barn y.e helder Rob.t Sergiant John Sergiant Rob.t Sygo Rychard Cobdock & thomas Lyster as by ther dede datyd y.e xxix day of Aprill anno R: R͠gs Henrici viij xxviij playnlyer aperith **And** a pece of lond cont.g iiij akers in Pakenham Feld caulyd Hardall betwen y.e lond of y.e monestery of bury of both p͠tis y.e est hed abutteth on y.e pathe caulid Malingmere & y.e west hed upon Thetsonrlwaye [*sic, i.e.,* Thetfordwaye] y.e whyche pece of lond with y.e apptenn͠cs I y.e forseid Edward Parker lately had to me & my heres of y.e gifte grante & confir-ma͠cn of Edmund Smyth Thomas Crysten John Lawrence otherwyse Smyth John barn y.e elder John Sergiant Robard Cobdok & Thomas Lyster as by ther dede datyd y.e xx daye of Aprill An° R: R͠gis Henrici viij xxviij **And** ij peces of lond lying in y.e towne & Felds of Pakenam the Furst Pece is extemyd for iij rods lying in Hardall Feld betwen y.e lond of Sir Thomas Jermyn Knyght ageynst y.e northe & y.e lond of y.e monestery of bury ageynst y.e southe y.e west hed abuttyng on y.e lond of y.e seid sr Thomas & y.e est hed upon malyngmere the second pece cont.g i Aker lying in y.e same feld betwen y.e lond of Edward Parker ageynst y.e southe and y.e lond of y.e monestery of bury ageynst y.e northe y.e west hed abuttyng on thetfordwaye y.e hest hed on y.e londe of dyvers men y.e whyche ij pecs with y.r apptnn͠cs I y.e seid John laurence al̓s Smyth of Pakenam lateli had of y.e gifte grant & confirma͠cn of John Cage vycar of Pakenam as by hys dede datyd y.e xxix day of Aprill anno R: R͠gis Henrici viij xxviij playnelier aperith **And** ij akers off erable lying in Stallmer Feld betwen y.e lond lately william Creston on y.e west & y.e lond lateli Robard Clerke ageynst y.e est y.e northe hede abuttyng on y.e pytell lately william gylle & y.e southe hed on y.e lond of y.e seyd

Robard Clerke ye whych ij pecs of lond I ye aforseid Edward Broke carpenter lateli had of ye gyfte grant & confirma̅c̅n of Edmund Smyth willyam Clerke Thomas Cage John Lyster Thomas Broke Thomas Crysten william Fyston Robard Sygo Robard Srgiant John Sergiant as by ther dede datyd ye xxviij daye of Aprill an^o R: R͠gis Henrici viij xxviij more playnelyer aperith **And** ij peces of lond in ye same Fyld of Pakeman ye one pece is extemyd for one aker lying betwen ye londs of ye monestery of bury lateli in tenure of william clerke ageynst ye west ye lond william [*sic*] ageynst ye hest ye west hed abuttyng on buri way & ye northe hed on ye lond of ye seid monestery ye second ext^d for haufe an aker & lying in akdall Feld betwen ye lond of John Barn on bothe sydis ye est hed abutt on ye lond of ye sayd John Barn on both sydis & ye est hed on ye lond of ye vicar of Pakenham ye whyche ij pecs of lond I ye forseid John Lyster lately hade of ye gifte grante & confirmacion of Edmund Smyth Thomas Cage Thomas Cristen John Laurence al̕s Smyth John Barn ye eld^r Robard Srgiant John Srgiant Robard Sygo Rychard Cobdok & Thomas Lyster as by ther dede datid at Pakenam ye xix day of Aprill An: R: R͠gs Henrici viij xxviij playnelyer aperith **And** one pece of arabill cont^g for iiij akers & one rode in Pakenham in wyndmyllfeld betwen ye lond of ye manor of Maulkyns Hall on ye south & ye lond late Thomas Strange ageynst ye northe ye west head abutt upon ye seid manor londs & ye east head on ye lond of ye seid Thomas Strange and ye londs of ye seid manor ye whych pece of erabill with ye apptenn̅c̅s we the forseid Henry Petit & william fiston lateli had of ye gifte grante & confirma̅c̅n of John lyster William Fysten Thomas Cristen John Cage Thomas Cage Thomas broke william Calabor John Barn & John laurence al̕s Smyth as by ther dede datid ye xxvi day of Aprill anno R: R͠gis Henrici viij xxviij more playnelier aperith **To have and to hold** all ye seid londs & tene̅m̅ts servyces woodes underwoodes hegs Rowys wais pathes & fedyngs with thapptnncs as is afore Rehersed to ye seid John Cage vycar of Pakenam & to his heres to the use and behoof of us Edmund Smyth Thomas Cage Edward Parker william west Thomas Cristen John lister ye elder William Fyston Benet Box John Barn ye elder Robard Sygo John Smyth william Calabor Thomas broke Edward broke Robt Srgiant John Srgiant Robt Cage William Pryor John Amy Rychard Cobdok Henry Cobdok & Thomas Sopor shall take receive & parceyve & for that intent & purpose that we the aforeseid Smyth Cage Parker Cristen west lyster fysten Box Barn Sygo Smyth Calabor Thomas & Edward Broke Robt & John Srgiant Robt Cage Prior Amy Rychard & Henri Cobdok & Thomas Sopor shall take receve & perceve ye issues profitts & emolyments of ye premisses from ye date of this present onto the end & time of xx^{ti} yeays be fulli endyd & expired ye whiche profitts so taken Rec^d & perceyvd shall convert to such use & uses charge & dyscharge as shall be thought mete expedyent or necessary by such as at what tyme ye seid towne or township of Pakenam shall be charged with any subsydy benevolence lone quinden tax or with ony eyd to the Kings warris generalli with ony manner of charge or imposycyons by what name or namys soever they be knowen shall be inabytants & dwellers personally on & in their proper londes & tenements whereof they shall be seised in their deme as of fee or fee tail **Provided always** that no foraner within the seid towne take any maner avantage or profit by or of the profites of the afor rehersed londs except it chance any man within the seid towne Resiant & abydynge be tenant by curtysy of Englond or any woman to be tenent in dower of ony londs or tenements within the towne of Pakenham whyche tenancy bi the curtesy or in dower shall take lyke avantage as they whyche shall have estate of inheritance as is aforseid **And** after the seid term of twenty yeays be full endyd to the onli proper use of us Edmund Smyth Thomas Cage Edward Parker William West Thomas Crysten John lister the elder william Benet Box John Barnes ye older Robt Sygo John Smyth william Calabor Thomas broke Edward broke Robt Syrgyant John Srgyant Robt Cage william Prior John Amy Richard Cobdok Henry Cobdok Thomas Sopor & of our heires for ever **Know** ye also furthermore that we the parties above have ordained set & apoyntyd Thomas Syer [*here follows a blank of an inch and a quarter, the preceding name not filling up the space which had been left for its insertion*] our faythfull & lawfull attorney to delyver our estate for us & eny of us on & in the premysses or eny part of them to the sayd John Cage Vycar accordyng to the purport strenght & effect of this present dede whyche estate so by them as our attorneyes we & ev'ry of us do aprove alow & admyt to be ferme & stabyll as well as if we ye above seid parties & every of us personalli had delyvyd ye said estate **In Witness Wherof** to thes presents we & evy of us haue set to our seales **Datyd** at Pakenam aforsaid the xxviij daye of September in the yer and raygne of oure sovraygne Lord Kynge henry the eyght the xxx^{ti}.

(Here occur nine seals.)

Endorsed : State & seizin given in presence of :—(N° 1.) William Hawys Stevyn Hawys Richard Baker Thomas with others. (N°s 2, 3, 4 & 5.) John Pryor Waltere Malstere Robt Beale with other. (N° 6.) [*Blank in orig.*] Noon gentylmā Lauerans Hunt Roberd Goche Wyllyam Blome Robert Telott and other. (N°s 7 & 8.) Roberd Whealbely Robert Beale John Neel with other. (N° 9.) Wylyā Borow Andrew Wygth John Oxforth John Roo the yonger with other.

The foregoing copies and abstracts have been most kindly made for me by the Rev. Charles William Jones, M.A., Vicar of Pakenham.—F. A. C.

Morgan Family.

James Morgan married to Elizabeth Lloyd March 26, 1814.
their Family,
Leslie Frederick born Feby 7, 1815 10 minutes to 12 night.   Died July 16, 1815.
James Horatio born June 28, 1816, 5 afternoon.
Hosier Leslie Frederick August 16, 1819 at 11 morning.

From a small Bible dated 1811, in my possession.—F. A. C.

Perceval Family.

Jany 26th 1756.

John the second Earl of Egmont was married in his own Chappel at Charlton in Kent at 12 o'Clock at Noon to his second Wife Miss Catherine Compton third Daughter of the late Honble Charles Compton Esqr Brother to James late Earl, & George the present Earl of Northampton. And Sister to Charles Compton (who afterwards succeeded his said Uncle George as Earl of Northampton).

October ye 1st 1756. between 4 & 5 o'Clock in the Morning the said Catherine Compton Countess of Egmont was brought to bed of a Son at Charlton aforesaid, who was Xtend there Octob. 4th 1756 by the name of Charles-George His sponsors being Charles Compton Esqr Eldest Brother to ye said Countess, (since Earl of Northampton) & George Earl of Northampton Uncle, and Lady Penelope Compton Aunt, to the said Countess of Egmont.

Saturday July 15th 1758. Lady Mary Perceval (Eldest daughter of the said Earl by the said Catharine Compton Countess of Egmont) was born at Charlton aforesaid. She was Xtend there on Monday the 7th of August following her Sponsors were Lady Margaret Compton her great Aunt, & Mrs Scott (now Lady Mary Scott) her Aunt, & Sr Berkeley Lucy Bart. her Great Grandfather.

Saturday 15 Decemb. 1759. Lady Anne Perceval (2^d daughter of the said Earl by the said Catharine Compton Countess of Egmont) was born at her Fathers House in Pallmall at a quarter after 8 of the Clock in the Morning. She was Xtend there by Dr Bearcroft Master of the Charter House on Friday Jany ye 11th 1760. Her Sponsors were the Honble George Townshend Esqr (Eldest Son & Heir Apparent to the Lord Visc^t Townshend, & to whom has since succeeded) Anne Wife of Charles Earl of Northampton, and Lady Anne Rushout—the former her Aunt, the latter her great Aunt. She died Aug^st ye 1st 1772 & was buried Aug^st 4th at Charlton in Kent.

Saturday 31 Jany 1761. Lady Charlotte Perceval (3^d daughter of the said Earl by the said Catharine Compton Countess of Egmont) was born at her Fathers House in St James's Square at 8 o'Clock in the Morning. She was Xtend there on ye 19th of Feby following and died the 23^d of ye same Month 3 Weeks & 2 days old—buried at Charlton in Kent.

Monday 1st Novemb^r 1762. Spencer Perceval second son of John Earl of Egmont (by his second Wife Catherine Compton Countess of Egmont Sister to Charles Compton Earl of Northampton) was born in Audley Square near Grosvenor Square London at half an hour past 7 o'Clock in ye Morning. He was Xtend there on Saturday the 27th of the same Month. His Sponsors were ye R^t Honble Sr John Rushout Bart. The Honble Spencer Compton his Mothers Brother (since by ye Death of his Brother Charles Earl of Northampton) The Lady Elizabeth Drummond his Mothers Sister, & Lady Baroness Chedworth Widow of the late Lord Chedworth.

Monday 12th Decemb. 1763. Lady Elizabeth Perceval (4th Daughter of the said Earl of Egmont, by the said Catharine Compton Countess of Egmont his second Wife, was born at her Fathers House at the Admiralty in the Parish of St Martins in the Fields at half an hour after

3 in the Afternoon. She was Xtend the 8th of Jany following 1764. Her Sponsors were the Lady Betty Germain, The Lady Ferrers Wife to George Townshend Eldest Son & Heir Apparent of ye Lord Visct Townshend (since Lord Townshend) & Admiral George Bridges Rodney Esqr.

Wednesday 26th June 1765. Henry Perceval, third Son of John Earl of Egmont by the said Catharine Compton Countess of Egmont his second Wife was born at his Fathers House at Turnham Green in the Parish of Chyswick in the County of Middlesex at twenty Minutes after six o'Clock in the afternoon. He was Xtend on Weñsday the 17th of July following, His Sponsors being The Rt Honble Sr John Cust Bart Speaker of the House of Commons, Henry Drummond Esqr Husband of Lady Elizabeth Sister to ye said Countess of Egmont, & Jane Countess of Northampton, Wife of Spencer now Earl of North-ampton Brother to ye said Countess of Egmont. he died July 27th 1772 & was buried at Charlton in Kent the 4th Augst.

Friday 4th Decemb. 1767. Lady Frances Perceval (fifth Daughter of the said Earl of Egmont Baron Lovell and Holland by Catharine Countess of Egmont his second Wife Sister of Spencer Compton now Earl of Northampton) was born at her Fathers House in Pallmall at half an hour after 3 in the Morning. She was there Xtend on Thursday the 31st of the said Month, Her Sponsors being the Rt Honble the Lord Boston, Frances Countess Dowager of Northampton (Widow of Earl George) and Mrs Middleton Wife of Mr Middleton of Chirke Castle, & Daughter of Sr John Rushout Bart.

Friday 17th March 1769. Margaret sixth Daughter of the said Earl of Egmont, Baron Lovell & Holland (by the said Catharine Countess of Egmont his 2d Wife Sister of Spencer Compton now Earl of North-ampton) was born at her Fathers House in Pallmall at 7 o'Clock in the Morning. She was there Baptiz'd on Friday the 14th of April following ; Her Sponsors being Allen Lord Bathurst, The Lady Margaret Compton her great Aunt, and Lady Catharine Wynne her Sister, viz another Daughter of the said Earl by his first wife, the Lady Catherine Cecil Dr of James the late, & Sister of James now Earl of Salisbury.

Thursday March 1st 1787.
Charles George Lord Arden was married to Miss Margaretta Eliza-beth Wilson, eldest Daughter of Sir Thomas Spencer Wilson Baronet, of Charlton in ye County of Kent, in the Chappel at Charlton House.

Wednesday 15 July 1789.
Margaretta Elizabeth, Lady Arden, was at a Quarter after one o'Clock in the Morning brought to Bed of a Daughter at the Admiralty in the Parish of St Martins in the Fields Westminster, and was Christened [blank in orig.] of August following by the Name of Catharine. Her Sponsors were, her Grandfather Sir Thomas Spencer Wilson Bart The Lady Elizabeth Drummond her great Aunt, & the Lady Wilson her Grandmother.

Friday 27th August 1790.
Helena Perceval 2d Daughter of Charles George, Lord Arden & Margaretta Elizabeth his Wife was born at her Fathers House at the Admiralty at half past Ten o'Clock at Night, & was Christened there the 27th of September following. Her Sponsors were Henry Drummond Esqr her Great Uncle, The Lady Mary Drummond, and the Honble Mrs Spencer Perceval, her Aunts.

Sunday the 20th of November 1791.

Charles-Thomas Perceval Son of Charles-George Lord Arden & Margaretta-Elizabeth his Wife was born at his Fathers House in the Admiralty at three o'Clock in ye Morning and was christened there the 24th of December following. His Sponsors were Charles Lord Compton, Sir Thomas-Spencer Wilson Bar^t and the R^t Honble Helena Countess Dowager of Mount-Cashell. Died 15th February 1793, buried at Charlton in Kent.

Saturday 13th April 1793.

John Perceval Son of Charles-George Lord Arden & Margaretta Elizabeth his wife was born at his Fathers House in the Admiralty a little before twelve o'Clock at Night and was christened there the 11th of May following. His Sponsors were John Earl of Egmont & the Honble Spencer Perceval his Uncles and the Lady Wilson his Grandmother.

Friday 14th March 1794.

George-James Perceval Son of Charles-George Lord Arden & Margaretta Elizabeth his Wife was born at his Fathers House in the Admiralty at eleven o'Clock at Night, and was Xten'd there the 17th of April following. His sponsors were George Earl of Leicester, James Gordon Junr of Moor Place in the County of Hertford Esqr, & the Lady Frances Perceval his Aunt.

30th July 1795.

Edward Perceval Son of Cha. Geo. Lord Arden & Margaretta Elizabeth his Wife was born at his Fathers House at Nork in the Parish of Banstead in ye County of Surrey, at a Quarter before nine o'Clock at Night, & was Xten'd there in September following. His Sponsors were The Honble Edward Perceval his Uncle Edward Finch Hatton Esqr and Lady Margaret Perceval his Aunt.

Christmas Day 1796. Charles-George Perceval, Son of Chas George Lord Arden and Margaretta-Elizabeth his Wife was born at his Fathers House in the Admiralty about 8 o'Clock in the Evening, and was christened there the 13th of February following. His Sponsors were Brownlow Lord Brownlow, Andrew Berkeley Drummond Esqre his Uncle, and Lady Frances Compton.

Caroline Perceval Daughter of Charles George Lord Arden and Margaretta Elizabeth his Wife was born at Nork House in the Parish of Banstead in the County of Surrey on Saturday the 30th of June 1798, about ½ past 3 o'Clock in the Afternoon, and was Christened there the 18th of August following. Her Sponsors were Sir John Trevelyan Bar^t Caroline Wife of Jo^s Lyons Walrond Esqr, & Frances Wife of Charles Drummond Esqr.

Friday 22^d November 1799. Arthur Philip Perceval Son of Chas George Lord Arden & Margaretta-Elizabeth his wife was born at his Fathers House at the Admiralty and was christened there on the 7th Day of January 1800. His Sponsors were Thomas Walpole Esqr The Revd Philip Perceval of Temple House in the County of Sligo, and Helena Countess of Kingston.

From a Bible in two volumes, " Oxford : Printed by Mr. Baskett, Printer to the University, MDCCXXXIX.," in the possession of Lucy, Countess of Egmont.—F. A. C.

RECEIPT SIGNED BY THE MINISTERS AND ELDERS OF THE FRENCH CHURCH OF ST. MARTIN ORGARS IN LONDON, DATED 21 OCTOBER 1742.

𝔑𝔲𝔪𝔟. *751.* Sam*l* Estere £*7 1c*
  752. D*o*—— 6

£*13 1c*

The   2 I   Day of   *October*   1742.

R*Eceived by* *us* *Ministers* *and* *Elders* *of the*
  French   *Church*   *of*   *St*   *Martin*   *Orgars*
of London as assigd by margin

  Horatio Walpole Esqr
Of the Right Honourable ~~Thomas Lord Onslow~~, *One of
the Four Tellers of His Majesty's Receipt of* Exchequer, *the
Sum of Thirteen pounds ten Shill*——

*in full of all former Directions, and for Six
Months Annuity, due at Michalmas   last past, of
Twenty Seaven   Pounds per Annum,
by Vertue of an Act of Parliament, (Entituled,* An Act for
continuing the Duties on Low Wines, and Spirits of
the First Extraction, and the Duties payable by Hawkers,
Pedlars and Petty Chapmen, and Part of the Duties on
Stampt Vellum, Parchment and Paper, and the late Duties on Sweets, and the One Third Sudsidy of Tonnage and
Poundage, and for Settling and Establishing a Fund thereby, and by the Application of certain Overplus Monies
and otherwise, for Payment of Annuities, to be sold for
raising a Supply to Her Majesty for the Service of the Year
1707, and other Uses therein express'd ;) *I say Received
by me* ——

C. *Dennaret.*

J. T. *Muysson Minist:*
D. *Beaufort, Min:*
Sr *Cubibely.*
Peter *Dobree.*
Ben: *Bonnet.*

The original of the above is in my possession.—F. A. C.

The ___ 21 ___ Day of ___ October ___ 1742.

REceived by us Ministers and Elders of the French Church of S.t Martin Orgars of London as asig. by margin

Horatio Walpole Esq.

Of the Right Honourable ~~Thomas Lord Onslow~~, One of the Four Tellers of His Majesty's Receipt of Exchequer, the Sum of *Thirteen pounds ten Shill.*

in full of all former Directions, and for *Six* Months Annuity, due at *Michaelmas* last past, of *Twenty Seaven* ___ Pounds per Annum, by Vertue of an Act of Parliament, (Entituled, An Act for continuing the Duties on Low Wines, and Spirits of the First Extraction, and the Duties payable by Hawkers, Pedlars and Petty Chapmen, and Part of the Duties on Stampt Vellum, Parchment and Paper, and the late Duties on Sweets, and the One Third Subsidy of Tonnage and Poundage, and for Settling and Establishing a Fund thereby, and by the Application of certain Overplus Monies and otherwise, for Payment of Annuities, to be sold for raising a Supply to Her Majesty for the Service of the Year 1707, and other Uses therein express'd ;) I say Received by me ———————

C. Demaret   *J. J. Muysson Minist*

D. Beaufort Min:

Peter Dobree

Wm Bonnet

Bonamy Family.

Jean Bonamy fils Jean naquit Le 18me Juin 1716 a Esté presentee au bateme Le 20me du d^t mois ayant po^r parrain Son oncle Pierre Bonamy & p^r marraine Marie Tupper Sa Grand Mere

Henry fils du d^t naquit Le 23 d'aout 1723 a Esté presenté au bateme Le 25me du d^t mois po^r parrain Le Sr Wm Henry po^r Le Sr Pierre Brock & pour marraine D^{me} Marie Graham po^r demoiselle Susanne Henry

Piere fils du d^t naquit Le 29 Juin a Esté presenté au bateme Le 2me Juillet 1722 ayant po^r parrain Le S^r piere Brock & po^r marraine mademoisselle Susanne Henry Sa tante

Mon fils Jenn Bonamy at né le 6e Decembre 1755 et batizé le 10e du même mois ayant pour parrains m^r Jean Brock fs W^m & son oncle Pierre Bonamy et pour maraine D^{me} nichelle De Carteret sa tante

(Decedé au Seigneur le 26e Mai 1806)

Mon fils Jean Bonamy né le 30eme Mars 1780, & batisé le 5eme Avril ensuivant a eu pour Parrains son Oncle Pierre Bonamy & son Cousin Phillipe De Carteret & pour Marraine D^{me} Elizabeth Bowden sa tante

Ma fille Marie Bonamy née le 21eme Juillet 1781, & batisée le 25eme du dit Mois, a eu pour Parrain Mr Elie Guerin Junr son Grand-Père, & pour Marraines, D^{lle} Marie Guerin & Esther Guerin ses Tantes

(Decedée au Seigneur le 4e Mai 1860)

Ma fille Anne Bonamy, née le 20eme Janvier 1784, & batisée le 24e du dit Mois, a eu pour Parrein Mr Pierre Allez des Prevots son Cousin & pour Marraines D^{me} Anne Moullin, & D^{lle} Esther Guerin ses Tantes

Ma fille Susanne Bonamy, née le 19e Mars 1788, & batisée le 26e du d^t Mois, a eu pour Parrein Mr Jean Bolger son Cousin & pour Marraines D^{me} Susanne Bonamy, & D^{lle} Anne Bonamy ses Cousines

(Decedée au Seigneur le 14e Juin 1862)

Ma fille Elise Bonamy, née le 19eme Avril 1791, & batisée le 27eme du dit Mois, a eu pour Parrain Mr Jean Collings son Cousin, & pour Marraines D^{me} Marie Olivier sa Grand Mere & Marie Bonamy sa Soeur

(Decedée au Seigneur le 6 Octobre 1798)

Mon fils Pierre Bonamy né le 30eme Mars 1794, & batisé le 6eme Avril ensuivant, a eu pour Parrains Mr Hellier Gosselin & Jean Bonamy Junr son frère & pour Marraine D^{me} Rachel Carey Gosselin

(Decedé au Seigneur le 16e Fevrier 1844 a Rio de Janeiro)

Henry fils de Jean Bonamy & d'Isabelle Vardon sa fe né le 7e d'Août 1817 & batisé le 20e du dit mois a eu pour Parrains Mr Henry Miller & son père & pour Marraine Dame Marie Bonamy sa grand mère

(Decedé au Seigneur le 22e Mai 1835)

Isabella Martha fille des susdits née le 25ᵉ Septembre 1818 & batisée le 15ᵉ Octobre a eu pour Parrain son père representant Mʳ Pierre Bonamy son oncle & pour marraines Dˡˡᵉ Marthe Vardon sa tante & Dˡˡᵉ Charlotte Marthe Le Marchant Mansell sa cousine

(Decédée au Seigneur le 23ᵉ Decembre 1822)

Jean Collings fils des susdits né le 4ᵉ Mai 1820, & bâtisé le 24ᵉ du dit mois a eu pour Parrains Jean Collings son Oncle & Bonamy Collings son Cousin & pour marraine Dᵐᵉ Marie Collings sa tante

Maria fille des susdits née le 26ᵉ Decembre 1821 & batisée le 15ᵉ Janvier 1822 a eu pour Parrain Mʳ Frederic Price Junʳ son oncle & pour marraines Dame Maria Price sa tante & Maria Price sa cousine

Louise fille des susdits né le 15ᵉ Novembre 1823 & bâtisée le 5ᵉ Decembre a eu pour Parrain son père réprésentant Mʳ Pierre Bonamy son oncle & pour marraines Dˡˡᵉ Susanne Bonamy sa tante & Dˡˡᵉ Eliza Margueritte Collings sa cousine

Isabella fille des susdits née le 21ᵉ Fevrier 1827 & bâtisée le 19ᵉ Mars a eu pour Parrain son père & pour marraines Dˡˡᵉ Marthe Vardon sa tante & Maria sa soeur

Marthe fille des susdits née le 2ᵉ Decembre 1829 & batisée 19ᵉ a eu pour Parrain son père & pour marraines Dˡˡᵉ Marthe Vardon sa tante & Dˡˡᵉ Louise Bonamy sa soeur

From a Bible in French, printed in Amsterdam in 1707, in two volumes folio, in my possession.—F. A. C.

Lettsom Family.

Indenture made 16 May 1796, between David Charles Bassett of Beckenham, co. Kent, of the one part, and John Coakley Lettsom of St. Giles', Camberwell, Doctor of Physick, of the other part, relating to land at Forest Hill, in Lewisham, co. Kent. Signature on fold of David Charles Bassett, and those of Samuel Lilley and Samˡ Jᵒ Lilley as witnesses.

Indenture made 21 September 1807, between John Coakley Lettsom of St. Giles', Camberwell, Doctor of Physic, of the one part, and Thomas Marriott Edwards of the same parish, Apothecary, of the other part, relating to land at Forest Hill, in Lewisham, co. Kent. Signature of John Coakley Lettsom on fold, and that of Sam: J. Lilley as witness.

John Coakley Lettsom

From the originals in the possession of Mrs. Colyer-Fergusson of Wombwell Hall, Gravesend.—F. A. C.

78

Paltock Family.

To all and singular persons as well Nobles as Gentles to whom theis presents shall come Wiłłm Segar Garter Principall King of Armes sendeth his due cõmendačons and greeting. Knowe yee that whereas Edward Paltock of Kingston vpon Thames in the County of Surrey gentleman, the sonne of Roƀt Paltock of the saide County and place gent: whoe beareth for his auncient Coat of Armes Asure an inscuchion with in an Vrle of cincq fieules gould: And wanting further for an ornament vnto his said Coat-Armoᵣ a convenient Creast or Cognisance fitt to be borne, Hath requested mee the said Garter by vertue, power and aucthority of myne Office to appoint hym suche a one, as hee may Lawfully bear wᵗʰoute wrongdoing, or preiudize to any others; The which his due request I the said Garter haue accordingly accomplisshed and graunted in manner, and forme following: That is saye, forth of a Wreath of his cullors on a hill vert, a Greyhound seiant sable flecked argent, collored or, Mantled, and doubled as in the margent ys depicted. All which Armes and Creast I the said Garter doe by theis p̃ntͻ ratify, confirme, gyue and graunt vnto the said Edward Paltock and to all the posterity of the said Robert Paltock ffather of the said Edward, to vse, beare, and shewe forth in Signett, sheild, ensigne, Coat-Armour, or otherwise, at his and theire free liberty and pleasure withoute lett, impediment, or interruption of any person or persons. In Witnes whereof I the said Garter haue herevnto sett my hand and seale of Office the fourteenth daye of Feabruary in the nynth yeare of the raigne of our soveraigne Lord James by the grace of God King of England, ffrance, and Ireland, Defendoᵣ of the faith, &c. and of Scotland the xliiijᵗʰ.

W Segar Garter princi pall King of Armes

*From the original Grant in my possession.—*F. A. C.

79

INDEX.

INDEX.

Abell.
 John, 57, 60.
 Nicholas, 60.
 Richard, 53, 54, 57, 58.
 William, 53.
Agas.
 John, 14.
Alexander.
 Lord High Stewart of Scotland, 30.
Allen.
 Mary, 10.
Allenby.
 Hynman, 23.
Alyor.
 John, 3.
Amers.
 George, 12.
Amy.
 John, 71, 72.
Amyce.
 —, 5.
Ancell.
 Mr., 5.
Andrewes, Andrews.
 Dorcas, 10.
 George, 10.
 John, 66.
 Mr., 3.
Angier.
 Samuel, 14.
 Thomas, 14.
Angur.
 Rev. Mr., 10.
Arden.
 Charles George, Lord, 74, 75.
 Margaretta Elizabeth, Lady, 74, 75.
Argar.
 John, 10.
Aspin.
 Rev. Harvey, 66.
Astley.
 Rev. John, 35.
Aubry.
 William, 54, 55.
Austen.
 Henery, 41.
 John, 40.

Awdeley.
 Thomas, 1.
Awecrofte.
 Peter, 6.
 —, 6.
Aylett.
 Will: 10.
Ayling.
 Eliz: 37.
 John, 37.

Bachiler.
 Margery, 3.
Bacon.
 John, 55.
Badwell.
 John, 55.
Baker.
 Ed: 10.
 Nathaniell, 10
 Richard, 72
Baldry.
 Anne, 30.
Ball, Balls.
 Ann, 14.
 Edward, 7.
 Na: 10.
 Samuell, 51.
Banyard.
 John, 53.
Barker.
 John, 66.
Barlee.
 Elizabeth, 2.
 Robert, 2.
Barn, Barnes.
 John, 68-72.
Barnard.
 John, 54.
Baron, Barown.
 John, 54, 58-61.
Barrett.
 Robert, 64, 65.
Barthorp.
 Anne, 33.
 Eliz: 31.
 John, 31, 33.

83

Baseley.
    Stephen, 15.
Basket.
    Mr., 75.
Bassett.
    David Charles, 78.
Bath.
    Henrie, 5.
    James, 5.
Bathurst.
    Allen, Lord, 74.
Bawde.
    John, 55.
Baxter.
    Edmond, 64, 65.
Bayllie.
    Mrs., 4.
Beadle.
    —, 8.
Beak, Beake.
    Anne, 10, 11.
Beale, Bele.
    Robert, 61, 72.
Bearcroft.
    Dr., 73.
Beaufort.
    D., 76.
Beaumont.
    B: 12.
Beckingham.
    Stephen, 13, 14.
Becon.
    Thomas, 55, 56.
Bell.
    Henry, 35.
    Rev. Philip, 35, 36.
Beman.
    Abell, 53.
    Maria, 53.
Benton.
    Aron, 6.
Best.
    William, 62.
Bird, Byrd.
    James Collis, 47.
    John, 53.
    Louisa Burroughes, 47.
Biggs.
    Rev. Robert, 25.
Blackborne.
    George, 65.
Blome.
    Wyllyam, 72.
Blomefield, Blumefeild.
    Edmond, 62, 63.
    Robert, 62, 63.
Bokenham.
    Lydia, 36.
    William, 36.

Boldero.
    Geo: 66.
    Roger, 66.
Bolger.
    John, 77.
Bonamy.
    Anne, 77.
    Elisa, 77.
    Henry, 77.
    Isabella, 78.
    Isabella Martha, 77.
    John, 77.
    John Collings, 78.
    Louisa, 78.
    Mary, 77, 78.
    Martha, 78.
    Peter, 77, 78.
    Susan, 77, 78.
Bonnett.
    Ben: 76.
Boradell, Borradale.
    Martha, 11.
Borow.
    Wylya, 12.
Boston.
    Lord, 74.
Botown.
    John, 58, 61.
Bott.
    Barbara, 5.
Boulton.
    Elizabeth, 46.
Bowden.
    Elizabeth, 77.
Box, Boxe, Boxxe.
    Benet, 69-71.
    John, 58-61.
    Robert, 58.
    William Benet, 72.
Bradbury.
    George, 1.
    Jane, 1.
    Dame Joane, 2.
    Mathew, 2.
    Robert, 1.
    Thomas, 1.
    William, 1.
Brand.
    J., 34.
Bridges.
    Ma: 4.
Bright.
    Henry, 62.
    Thomas, 64.
    William, 62.
Brock.
    John, 77.
    Peter, 77.
Brockwell.
    John, 10.

Choppin.
  Richard, 2.
Chunn.
  Joseph, 6.
  —, 6.
Church.
  Elizabeth, 14.
  Sarah, 17.
Churrie.
  Dorothie, 6.
  John, 6.
Chylston.
  John, 53.
Clarke, Clerk, Clerke.
  Benj: 59.
  John, 54, 62, 64, 65.
  Richard, 62.
  Robert, 53-55, 58, 70, 71.
  T., 59-61.
  Thomas, 61.
  William, 54-59, 61, 69-71.
Clement.
  John, 53.
  Mary, 53.
Clifford.
  Elizabeth, 2.
  Dame Elizabeth, 2.
  Sir Robert, 2.
  Thomas, 2.
Cobdok.
  Henry, 69, 71, 72.
  John, 60.
  Nicholas, 61.
  Richard, 56, 57, 59, 60, 61, 69-72.
  Robert, 56, 57, 59, 70.
Cocke.
  William, 11.
Cockshutt.
  Stephen, 9.
  Thomas, 9.
Codd.
  George, 63.
Cok.
  John, 53.
Cole.
  Denney, 18.
  Edward Wright, 18.
  Elizabeth, 17, 18.
  John, 17, 18.
  Nathaniel, 17.
  Samuel, 17, 18.
  Sarah, 17, 18.
  Sarah Martha, 17, 18.
  Thomas, 17.
  Thomas Springar, 18.
Colepeper.
  Anne, 37.
  Sir Anthony, 37.
Collings.
  Bonamy, 78.
  Eliza Margaret, 78.
  John, 77, 78.
  Mary, 78.

Colyer-Fergusson.
  Mrs., 78.
Compton.
  Catharine, Countess of Egmont, 73, 74.
  Hon. Charles, 73.
  Charles, Earl of Northampton, 73.
  Charles, Lord, 75.
  Lady Frances, 75.
  Frances, Countess of Northampton, 74.
  George, Earl of Northampton, 73.
  James, Earl of Northampton, 73.
  Jane, Countess of Northampton, 74.
  Lady Margaret, 73, 74.
  Lady Penelope, 73.
  Hon. Spencer, Earl of Northampton,
    73.
Coney, Cony.
  Mary, 17.
  Sutton Jo: 66.
Cook, Cooke.
  John, 62, 63.
  Ralfe, 62.
  Richard, 62.
  Robert, 18, 19, 55.
  Roger, 62.
  William, 62.
Cooper.
  Christopher, 12.
Copenger.
  Robert, 55.
Copin.
  Widd^w, 63.
Copping.
  Edmund, 66.
  Thomas, 66.
Cordell.
  Sir Arthur, Bt., 62.
  Sir William, 3.
Cornelius.
  Tho: 12.
Coton, Cotton.
  Alexandrina, 39.
  Arthur Annesley, 38.
  Arthur Annesley Valentia, 39.
  Arthur Henry Buller, 39.
  Charles Bowland, 39.
  Charles William, 39.
  Harriot, 39.
  Harriot Powell, 39.
  Laura Susan, 39.
  Sigesmond, 1.
Cotysins.
  John, 57.
Courtman.
  —, 10.
Cox.
  John, 9.
Crayford.
  Guy, 2.
Creme.
  Henry, 55.

86

Creston, Cristen, Cristyn, Crysten, Cryston, Crystyn.
    Thomas, 58-61, 68-72.
    William, 54, 58.
Crisp, Crispe.
    John, 49-51, 63.
Crooke.
    Richard, 53.
Croxon.
    Randall, 10.
Cubibely.
    Sr, 76.
Cuddon.
    Thomas, 25.
Culverwell.
    Mr., 3.
Curtis.
    Martyn, 7.
Cust.
    Sir John, Bt., 74.
Cutting.
    Mary, 17.

Dallinger.
    Robart, 33.
    Sarah, 33.
Davison.
    Mr., 10.
Dawkens.
    Elizabeth, 7.
    Mary, 7.
    Peter, 7.
    —, 7.
De Carteret.
    Michelle, 77.
    Philip, 77.
Dencrosse.
    William, 58.
Denham.
    Mary Ann, 20.
Dennaret.
    C., 76.
Derrick.
    Mr., 3.
Des Prevots.
    Allez Peter, 77.
Dewes.
    Sir Simond, 64.
Dickenson.
    Christopher, 11.
    Thomas, 11.
Dobree.
    Peter, 76.
Doe.
    William, 66.
Downes.
    Humphry, 7.

Drummond.
    Andrew Berkeley, 75.
    Charles, 75.
    Lady Elizabeth, 73, 74.
    Frances, 75.
    Henry, 74.
    Lady Mary, 74.
Drury.
    John, 69.
Duckett.
    William, 5.
Dunbar.
    Thomas, 14.
Dyer.
    Benjamin, 11.
Dygby.
    Benjamyn, 1.
Dykes.
    Mr., 3.

Earle.
    Margaret, 5.
Easterson.
    Mary, 31.
    Thomas, 31.
Edgiott.
    James, 3.
Edward IV.
    King of England, 53, 54.
Edwards.
    Easter, 17.
    Mary, 17.
    Thomas Marriott, 78.
Egmont.
    Catherine, Countess of, 73, 74.
    John, Earl of, 73-75.
    Lucy, Countess of, 75.
Eldergate.
    Elyanor, 2.
Eldred.
    John, 9, 10.
    Margaret, 10.
Elizabeth.
    Queen of England, 2, 3, 49.
Elliott, Ellyott.
    John, 3.
    Rose, 3.
Estere.
    Saml, 76.
Etheridge.
    Gwyn, 35, 36.
Eve.
    Anne, 3.
    Marie, 3.
    Suzan, 3.
    Thomas, 3.
Everet.
    Samuel, 10.
Evett.
    William, 64.

Felde.
　　Richard, 2.
Felton.
　　Nicholas, 12.
Ferrers, Feryars.
　　Lady, 74.
　　Richard, 61.
Ferwe.
　　George, 55, 56.
Finch-Hatton.
　　Edward, 75.
Fitson, Fysoon, Fysten, Fyston.
　　John, 55, 58.
　　William, 56, 58, 59, 68-71.
Fitzherbert.
　　Elizabeth, 1.
　　Humfrey, 1.
　　John, 1.
　　Robert, 1.
Fletcher.
　　Henry, 15.
Flowerdew.
　　Sarah, 35.
Fludyer.
　　Maria, 22.
　　Sir Saml Brudenell, Bt., 21, 22.
Ford.
　　Mr., 7.
Fordham.
　　Benedict, 54, 57, 60.
　　Thomas, 58, 60.
Fouler, Fowler.
　　George, 12.
　　John, 53.
Fox.
　　John, 17, 25.
Foyle.
　　Edward, 13.
Freeborne.
　　John, 3.
Freind, Friend.
　　Ann, 44.
　　Dorothy, 12.
　　Edward, 45.
　　Elizabeth, 44, 46.
　　George, 41, 42, 44-46.
　　George Twyman, 46.
　　Henrietta, 46.
　　Henry, 44.
　　Rev. Henry, 42.
　　James, 45.
　　John, 42, 44, 46, 47.
　　Margaret, 46.
　　Margary, 41.
　　Mary, 42, 46.
　　Mary Ann, 46.
　　Phœbe, 42.
　　Richard, 12.
　　Sarah, 42, 44.
Freston.
　　Anthony, 35, 36.

Fullere.
　　John, 56, 57.
Fysch, Fysh, Fyssh, Fysshe.
　　John, 53, 54.
　　Ralph, 58.
　　Thomas, 54.
　　William, 55, 58, 69.

Gage.
　　Edward, 14.
Gall.
　　Robert, 19.
　　Mary, 19.
Gambon, Gambown.
　　Robert, 53, 54.
　　Thomas, 57-61.
Gardener.
　　Sir Robert, 62.
Garrat, Garrett.
　　John, 13.
　　Mr., 52.
Garrod.
　　Margaret, 34.
Gate.
　　Dorothy, 1.
　　Sir Geffrey, 1, 2.
　　Sir Henry, 3.
　　Joceline, 4, 7.
　　Peter, 4.
　　—, 7.
George III.
　　King of England, 66, 67.
Germain.
　　Lady Betty, 74.
Gibb, Gybbe.
　　John, 2.
　　Mr., 65.
Gilfird.
　　John, 65.
Gill.
　　John, 12.
Gilly.
　　Clement, 62.
Gilson.
　　Alenton, 20.
　　Alenton William, 20.
　　Alice, 20.
　　Ann, 20.
　　Beatar, 20.
　　Eleanor, 20.
　　George, 20.
　　Hannah, 20.
　　Henry, 20.
　　John, 20.
　　Mary, 20.
　　Nathaniel, 66.
　　Rebekah, 20.
　　Sarah, 20.
　　Thomas, 20.
　　Wm, 20.
　　Zadok, 20.

Glascok.
    —, 2.
Glave.
    Hughe, 3.
Glovere.
    John, 55.
Goare.
    John, 41.
Goche.
    Roberd, 72.
Godwin.
    George, 15.
Golding, Goulding.
    John, 7.
    William, 66.
Gooddy.
    Phillis, 3.
Goodson.
    Rev. John, 55, 58.
Gordon.
    James, 75.
Gosselin.
    Hellier, 77.
    Rachel Carey, 77.
Graham.
    Mary, 77.
Gray, Grey.
    Mary, 48.
    Susan, 46.
    Thomas, 46, 48.
Green.
    Macklin, 14.
Gretom.
    Mary, 17.
Gretton.
    John, 44.
    Sarah, 44.
Griffen, Gryffyn.
    Humfrey, 2.
    John, 56.
Gross.
    Ann, 26.
    Anna Eliza Emily, 26.
    Anne Eliza Maria, 26.
    Mary, 29.
    Mary Rebecca, 29.
    Samuel, 26.
    Samuel Chilton, 26, 29.
    Woolnough, 26.
Grymesby.
    William, 56, 57.
Guerin.
    Elie, 77.
    Esther, 77.
    Mary, 77.
Guma . .
    John, 61.
Gylle.
    William, 54, 58, 70.

Hacke.
    Robert, 8.
Hadley.
    George, 2.
Hall, Haull.
    John, 58.
    Richard, 69.
Hamond.
    Henrie, 5.
Hampson.
    Ann, 7.
Harlakenden.
    Richard, 9.
Harper.
    Eliz: 31.
    John, 31.
Harris.
    Dorothie, 5.
    Richard, 5.
Hart.
    Thomas, 69.
Hasell.
    John, 62.
Hatfeild, Hatfield.
    Edward, 46, 64.
    Sarah, 46.
Hatton.
    Henry, 10.
    See also Finch-Hatton.
Hawys.
    John, 55-57.
    Stevyn, 72.
    William, 55, 72.
Haynes.
    He : 11.
    Hezekiah, 9.
Hebden.
    Alice, 24.
    Arthur, 24.
    Henry Bernard, 24.
Hedge.
    Henrye, 51.
Henry.
    Susan, 77.
    William, 77.
Henry VII.
    King of England, 54-56.
Henry VIII.
    King of England, 1, 2, 56-61, 68-72.
Herne.
    John, 54.
    William, 54.
Hert, Herte.
    John, 54, 58, 59.
    William, 53, 54, 58.
Heynys.
    Rev. John, 44.
Hide.
    Thomas, 5.
Highiam.
    Ann, 7.

Hills.
    Joseph, 6.
Hoggesdon.
    Sir Georde, 2.
Holdder.
    Thomas, 54.
Holland.
    John, Lord, 74.
Hollingworth.
    Captain, 66.
    William, 66.
Holmes.
    Rebecca, 36.
Homan.
    John, 13.
Hoo.
    John, 55, 56.
    Robert, 57.
Houghton.
    Mr., 65.
Howard.
    Ann, 7, 27.
    Robert, 27.
    Sarah, 27.
Howe.
    Mathewe, 51.
Hudson.
    Tobias, 4.
    William, 4.
Huett.
    Tho: 14.
Hull.
    Susan, 51.
Humberston.
    Richard, 15.
Humfry, Humphrey, Humphry.
    Edmund, 61-63.
Hunt.
    John, 58.
    Lauerans, 72.
Husbands.
    Edward, 14.
Hussey.
    Thomas, 12.
Hye.
    William, 53.
Hyndes.
    Elizabeth, 21.

Ingolde.
    John, 2.
Ive.
    Simon, 53.

Jackson.
    Christopher, 9.
Jacob.
    Edmund, 66.
    John, 66.
James I.
    King of England, 62, 79.

Jannings.
    James, 67.
    Robert, 66.
Jaskin.
    John, 64.
Jaslin, Jocelin, Joceline, Jocelyn, Jocelyne,
    Josceline, Joscelyn, Joscelyne, Joselin,
    Joseling, Joselyn, Joselyne, Joshlyn,
    Joslin, Josling, Joslinge, Joslyn, Joslynn,
    Josselin, Josselyn, Josslin, Jossling,
    Josslyn.
    Amy, 10.
    Ann, 8.
    Anna, 4, 6.
    Anne, 1, 2, 4, 7-15.
    Annis, 6.
    Anthony, 4, 15, 16.
    Arthur, 8, 12, 14, 15.
    Catherine, 16.
    Cecily, 1.
    Christopher, 12.
    Daniell, 8.
    Deborah, 16.
    Dorothy, 1, 4, 7.
    Dame Dorothy, 2, 3.
    Edmond, 8, 16.
    Edward, 2-4, 8, 10, 13.
    Elizabeth, 3-5, 7-10, 12, 14-16.
    Ellin, 6.
    Frances, 5, 8, 15.
    Francis, 5, 8, 15, 16.
    Gabryell, 1.
    Geffery, 1, 4.
    George, 1, 13.
    Hon. George, 16.
    Giles, 8.
    Grace, 6, 7, 16.
    Hannah, 9.
    Henry, 2-5, 7, 12, 15, 16.
    Hezechiah, 10.
    Hugh, 13.
    Humfrey, 3.
    Jacob, 16.
    James, 13, 14.
    Jane, 1-5, 10, 11, 13, 15.
    Dame Jane, 13.
    Joane, 3, 6.
    John, 1-6, 8-13, 15, 16.
    Joseph, 4.
    Margaret, 3, 5, 6, 13, 16.
    Maria, 5.
    Martha, 8, 11, 13, 14.
    Mary, 3, 4-9, 14, 15.
    Matthew, 6, 7.
    Mr., 3.
    Nathaniel, 4, 6, 9, 10.
    Peter, 6.
    Philip, 1, 5, 12.
    Phillis, 3.
    Ralph, 1, 3, 4, 6, 7, 15.
    Sir Raufe, 2.
    Rebecca, 6, 8.
    Richard, 2, 4-8, 10, 11, 16.
    Robert, 11.
    Sir Robert, 9, 13.

Jaslin, &c., *continued*.
    Rose, 14.
    Samuel, 14.
    Sarah, 5-7, 11, 13.
    Simon, 3-7, 13.
    Sorrell, 5.
    Sir Strange, Bt., 13.
    Strange, 13.
    Susanna, 5.
    Theoball, 8.
    Thomas, 1-3, 5, 6, 10, 11, 13, 15.
    Sir Thomas, 2, 3, 4.
    Ursula, 8.
    William, 12, 13.

Jeaffreson.
    Anne, 33.
    Elizabeth, 33.
    John, 33.
Jeffery.
    John, 12.
Jegon.
    Rob, 14.
Jenney.
    Edmund, 35.
    Elizabeth, 35.
    Marianne, 35, 36.
    William, 35, 36.
Jennings.
    Sarah, 46.
    Upton, 46.
Jermen, Jermyn.
    Sir Thomas, 62, 69, 70.
Jervis, *see* White-Jervis.
Jeve.
    John, 11.
Johnson.
    Grace, 7.
    Robert, 7.
Jones.
    Ame, 52.
    Benjamin, 52.
    Rev. Charles, 67.
    Rev. Charles William, 67, 72.
    Dina, 52.
    George, 52.
    Rev. Harry, 68.
    Joseph, 52.
    Samuell, 52.
    Sarah, 52.
    Susanna, 52.
Jordan, Jorden, Jurden.
    Abraham, 63, 64.
    Nathaniell, 62-64.

Keame.
    William, 11.
Kelton.
    Jane, 2, 3.
    Richard, 2.
Kendricke.
    Anne, 6.
    John, 6.

Kerby, Kirby.
    Joane, 40.
    John, 40.
    Paull, 40.
    Thomas, 40.
Kerington.
    Roger, 65.
Kerrich.
    Barbara, 35, 36.
    Rev. Samuel, D.D., 35, 36.
King.
    Martha, 11.
    Susan, 11.
    Susanna, 11.
Kingston.
    Helen, Countess of, 75.
Kisser.
    Marthy, 17.
Knava.
    Will: 5.
Knightsbridge.
    Anthony, 9.

Lambe.
    Marye, 4.
    —, 4.
Lance.
    Phillis, 5.
    William, 5.
Lane.
    James, 55.
Langham.
    Robert, 66.
Lany.
    Ann, 64.
    Rev. Benjamin, 66.
Lauerans, Lauerawns, Laurence, Lawrance,
    Lawrens.
    John, 57-61, 68-71.
Lawrie, Lawry.
    James, 5.
    Johan, 5.
Lay, Ley.
    Elizabeth, 15.
    Timothy, 15.
Lea, Lee.
    Joane, 3.
    Lyddia, 3.
    Nathaniell, 12.
Leach.
    Howard John, 27.
    John Dennington, 27.
    Sarah, 27.
    Sophia Bedwell, 27.
Leicester.
    George, Earl of, 75.
Leigh.
    Tho: 11.
Le Janders.
    Sarah, 17, 18.
    Susan, 18.

Middleton.
    Mr., 74.
    Mrs., 74.
Miller.
    Henry, 77.
Millward.
    John, 5.
Mockett.
    William, 39.
Monyngs.
    Richard, 49.
Morgan.
    Elizabeth, 72.
    Hosier Leslie Frederick, 72.
    James, 72.
    James Horatio, 72.
    Leslie Frederick, 72.
Moullin.
    Anne, 77.
Mount-Cashell.
    Helena, Countess of, 75.
Murton.
    Annis, 5.
    Charity, 5.
    Henry, 5.
    John, 5.
Muysson.
    J. T., 76.
Mygar.
    Edward, 2.

Neagoose.
    Mr., 3.
Neame.
    Ann, 42, 44.
    Charlotte, 42.
    Elizabeth, 44.
    Francis, 44.
    James, 42, 44.
    John, 39, 44.
    Maria, 42.
    Martha, 39.
    Mary, 44.
    Sarah, 42.
    William, 44.
Neel.
    John, 61, 72.
Negus.
    John, 10.
Nell, Nelle.
    John, 58, 59, 69.
Newman.
    Sir Robert, 2.
Noon.
    —, 72.
North.
    Stephen, 9.

Northampton.
    Anne, Countess of, 73.
    Charles, Earl of, 73.
    Frances, Countess of, 74.
    George, Earl of, 73, 74.
    James, Earl of, 73.
    Jane, Countess of, 74.
    Spencer, Earl of, 73, 74.
Norton.
    Augustus Addington, 25.
    Catharine, 25.
    Eleanor Douglas, 25.
    Rev. William Addington, 25.
    William Douglas, 25.
Norwiche.
    Robert, 1.
Note.
    Robert, 55, 56.
Numan.
    Richard, 55.
Nunne.
    John, 55, 56.
Nussell.
    Ebenezer, 44.
    Sarah, 44.
Nuttall.
    Charles, 3, 4.
    James, 3, 4.
    Marye, 4.
    Thomas, 4.

Olivier.
    Mary, 77.
Onslow.
    Thomas, Lord, 76.
Osbourn.
    Thomas, 65.
Outlaw.
    Henry, 68.
Overton.
    Elizabeth, 8.
Oxforth.
    John, 72.
Oxley.
    Elizabeth, 14.

Paine.
    John, 22.
    Mary, 22.
Pake.
    Christopher, 3.
Palfrey.
    Phillip, 63.
Palmar.
    Edward, 7.
Paltock.
    Edward, 79.
    Robert, 79.
Parey.
    John, 6.

Quintin.
    Anna, 28.
    Jonathan, 28.

Rainbird.
    John, 65.
Ram.
    Mary, 10.
Ramsdale.
    Susan, 10.
Ravens.
    Nicholas, 10.
Ray.
    Rev. William Carpenter, 66.
Reeves.
    Ann, 64.
Rery.
    Rev. Robert, 56.
Reynberd.
    Robert, 57.
    Thomas, 57, 59.
Reynghold.
    Richard, 57.
Rice.
    Hugh, 13.
Rickard.
    Thomas, 8.
Roberts.
    Arthur Annesley Powell, 38.
    Elizabeth, 37, 38.
    William, 37, 38.
Robinson.
    Anne, 11.
    Elizabeth, 11.
    John, 11.
    Mary, 11.
    Roskana, 11.
    William, 11.
Rochell.
    William, 4.
Rocheman.
    John, 56.
Roderham.
    —, 19.
Rodney.
    Admiral George Bridges, 74.
Rodwell.
    Joshua, 29.
    Mary Jane, 29.
    Sarah Bredell, 29.
Roger, Rogers.
    John, 17, 18.
    Mr., 3.
    Robert, 13.
Roo.
    John, 72.
Roos.
    John, 58.
Roschebrok, Roshebrok, Rosshebrok.
    George, 56.
    John, 55, 57, 58.

Rose.
    Edward, 55.
    Thomas, 53-56.
    William, 55, 56.
Rossetti.
    Gabriel Chas Dante, 47.
Rous.
    Benjamin, 11.
    John, 53.
Rushout.
    Lady Anne, 73.
    Sir John, Bt., 73, 74.
Rust.
    Giles, 65.
Rycheman.
    John, 57.

St. Edmunds.
    Richard, Abbot of, 53.
Salisbury.
    James, Earl of, 74.
Sams.
    Edward, 3.
    Elizabeth, 3.
    Henry, 3.
Sandby.
    Rev. George, 35.
Sargant, Sargaunt, Sergant, Sergeant,
  Sergeaunt, Sergiant, Sergyant, Serjant,
  Serjaunt, Serjawnt, Srgiant, Srygant,
  Syrgyant.
    John, 58-61, 68-72.
    Nicholas, 55.
    Peter, 62.
    Robert, 55, 56, 58-61, 68-72.
    William, 54, 58.
Saunder.
    Edmund, 5.
Sawer.
    Jane, 21.
    John, 21.
Sayer.
    Daniel, 35, 36.
Scott, Skott.
    Alfred Joice, 48.
    Elizabeth, 48.
    John, 57, 59.
    Lady Mary, 73.
    Robert, 56.
    William, 48.
Sculford.
    John, 62.
Sculthorpe.
    John, 63.
Seamor.
    —, 8.

Strange, Straunge.
    Henry, 53.
    John, 13.
    Roger, 69.
    Thomas, 71.
    William, 13.
Strivens.
    Mary, 44.
    Nicholas, 44.
    Sarah, 44.
Strutt.
    Elizabeth, 17.
Stubbs.
    Rev. Thomas, 35, 36.
Stubing.
    Dorothy, 7.
Stubbins.
    Richard, 4.
Sumner.
    Elizabeth, 3.
Surry.
    Sarah, 17.
Susshe.
    Henry, 2.
Sydey.
    Wallgrave, 4.
    William, 4.
    —, 4.
Syer.
    Thomas, 59, 72.
    William, 65.

Tabor.
    Mr., 10.
Taddy.
    Edward, 46.
    Mary, 46.
Taynetor.
    William, 3.
Tayspill.
    Anne, 14.
    Benjamin, 14.
    Martha, 14.
    Thomas, 14.
Telott.
    Robert, 72.
Thompson.
    Thomas, 7.
Thornhill.
    Thomas, M.P., 68.
Thorneaton, Thorneton, Thornton.
    Edmond, 3.
    James, 45.
    Jone, 3.
Tighe-Gregory.
    Rev. A., 34.
    Katharine Mary Josephine, 30.
    Margaret, 34.
Till.
    Elizabeth, 7.

Todd.
    Ann, 7.
    Ratcliffe, 7.
Tomlin.
    Cornelius, 45.
    Elizabeth, 45.
    Harriet, 47.
    James, 43.
    Jane, 43.
    John, 43.
    Robert, 47.
    Susannah, 43.
    William, 43.
Tomson.
    Widd^w, 64.
Tomys.
    Edward, 59.
Towler.
    John, 62-64.
    William, 62-64, 66.
    Xtopher, 62.
Townshend.
    George, Lord, 73, 74.
Trevelyan.
    Sir John, Bt., 75.
Trigge.
    Roger, 2.
Tubb.
    John, 5.
Tupper.
    Mary, 77.
Turner.
    John, 11.
    Mary, 11.
Twisden.
    Dame Catherine, 16.
Tyrell.
    Sir John, 1.
Tysoo.
    Rev. George, 55, 56.

Underdown.
    Ann, 41.
    Thos, 41.

Van Kamp.
    John, 35, 36.
    Susanna Maria, 35.
    Tabitha, 35.
Vardon.
    Isabel, 77.
    Martha, 78.
Veer.
    Sir John, 2.
Vertue.
    Samuel, 30.
Vintcent.
    Widd^w, 63.

www.ingramcontent.com/pod-product-compliance
Lightning Source LLC
Chambersburg PA
CBHW080000280326
41935CB00013B/1696